Man with a Load of Mischief

a new MUSICAL

Book by
BEN TARVER

Lyrics by
JOHN CLIFTON & BEN TARVER

Music by
JOHN CLIFTON

Man With a Load of Mischief Copyright 1966, 2011 by John Clifton, Donald H. Goldman and Ben Tarver.

All Rights Reserved. International Copyright Secured

No part of this book, including text, lyrics, and graphics, may be reproduced in any form or by any means, electronic or mechanical, including photocopying, recording, or by an information storage and retrieval system, without written permission in writing from the Publisher. Unauthorized copying, arranging, adapting, recording or public performance is an infringement of copyright. Infringers are liable under the law.

Publication date, Revised Edition: April 2011
ISBN 978-0-9760846-6-2

Additional copies and information:
Visit the show's Web site at *MischiefTheMusical.com* for further information and to order additional copies of this script, Piano-Vocal Score and CD Recording.

Performance rights licensed by SAMUEL FRENCH, New York

Foley Square Books
P. O. Box 20548
Park West Station
New York, NY 10025

Donald H. Goldman presents

Man with a Load of Mischief

a new MUSICAL

Music by
JOHN CLIFTON

Lyrics by
JOHN CLIFTON AND BEN TARVER

Book by
BEN TARVER

Based upon the play **The Man With a Load of Mischief**
by Ashley Dukes

Directed by TOM GRUENEWALD
Musical Direction by SANDE CAMPBELL
Choreography by NOEL SCHWARTZ
Scenery and Lighting by JOAN LARKEY
Costumes by VOLAVKOVA

— Original Cast —

THE INNKEEPER	Tom Noel
THE WIFE	Lesslie Nicol
THE MAN	Reid Shelton
THE MAID	Alice Cannon
THE LORD	Raymond Thorne
THE LADY	Virginia Vestoff

First performance November 6, 1966
Jan Hus Playhouse, New York

CAST
(In Order of Appearance)

THE INNKEEPER	A small man, rather stout, good-natured, likes his drink. Fifties to sixties. (Character voice)
THE WIFE	A jolly woman but with more drive than her husband, sharp tongued. Fifties. (Character soprano)
THE MAN	Quiet, enigmatic. The Lord's manservant. Forties. Charismatic but not conventionally handsome. (Tenor or Lyric Baritone)
THE MAID	Pretty but rather flighty, well aware of her attractiveness. In service to the Lady. Early twenties. ("Show" voice/Mix)
THE LORD	A dashing, handsome gentleman, friend of the Prince. Rather a snob. Twenties to early thirties. (Baritone)
THE LADY	Beautiful, proud — a former actress, mistress to the Prince. Late twenties to thirties. (Mezzo Soprano)

TIME
Early in the nineteenth century

PLACE
England, a wayside inn

NOTES ON MAN WITH A LOAD OF MISCHIEF

When this musical opened in November of 1966 the United States was in turmoil — race confrontations across the South, political assassinations and massive unrest among the young. A light hearted romantic musical would seem out of place during a period of anti-establishment sentiment. Nevertheless *"Mischief"* attracted a large and loyal audience that has lasted for half a century. The strong feminist sentiment of the play it is based on must have had something to do with that.

The play it is taken from was written by Ashley Dukes, one of London's most controversial drama critics during the turbulent 1920's. Dukes was an ardent Fabian and a strong advocate of the writing and views of George Bernard Shaw. Both men were not only socialists but also outspoken feminists. Shaw's Pygmalion is a better-known example of that position, and it too, of course, was the basis for a romantic, lyrical musical. And as with *My Fair Lady* few if any of the reviews that followed the opening night of *Man With a Load of Mischief* mentioned feminism.

The story of the play takes place in the Empire period circa 1820. This choice was certainly deliberate, for this was also a period of anti-establishment and feminist sentiment. The famous romantic poets and writers of the time – Byron, Keats, Shelley, Coleridge, *et al* — were political activists. People of that ilk (and there were many of them) were often reviled, fined and even jailed. When Victoria ascended the throne she and her ministers did everything in their power to squelch this uprising, thus the outward stodginess of the Victorian Age and the persecution of people like Oscar Wilde.

The action of *Man With a Load of Mischief* is centered around a Lady of a certain reputation, the mistress of the Prince of Wales, who runs away from court, determined to live a life of her own at any cost. The nobleman who pursues her clearly states, "Such cattle are dangerous." He is determined to apprehend her and take her back to the Prince. She finds a champion in the Lord's manservant who is willing to take the risk of helping her, even of joining her in her flight. This was no simple romantic tangle. They were risking their lives. In the eyes of the establishment they were guilty of treason. The manservant could have been hanged. One did not challenge the heir to the British throne in those days without suffering the consequences.

Despite the serious theme, the audience when leaving a performance of *Man With a Load of Mischief* is upbeat, cheerful and humming one of the many memorable tunes. Still, are they not saying to themselves, "Good for her! Good for him! That will teach the high and mighty a lesson!"

—B. T.

ABOUT CASTING

This is a show dealing with appearances. People are not always what they seem—a person's outside doesn't always reveal what is inside. In *Man With a Load of Mischief* it is especially important to cast the Man and the Lord correctly. The Man should *not* be dashing and obviously handsome. While ultimately charismatic and mysterious, he should seem at first to be an ordinary servant—reserved, somewhat older than the typical leading man. The Lord, on the other hand is *not* a silly fop, but a young, attractive nobleman. If the opposite is true, and the Man is young and handsome, and the Lord an obvious old twit, much of the meaning of the show goes out the window: Things then *are* what they seem!

When the Man first enters, the audience should not notice him very much. The Lord must appear to be the obvious partner for the Lady. Otherwise, there is no surprise as we discover that the Man runs deep and the Lord is but a superficial snob. Also, we should feel when the Lady is attracted to the Man that she seeks depth of character over external appearance.

Casting the other roles is not quite as tricky, but there are some considerations. The Lady and Maid should both be attractive in their own ways, but one must guard against conventional characterizations. All the persons in the play eventually reveal something surprising about themselves that separates them from "stock" figures. The Innkeeper and the Wife ideally should be substantially older than the other characters. The Wife should not have an ounce of glamour about her. The Innkeeper, while he obviously likes his gin at the end of the workday, is *not* an old drunk, as some have misguidedly portrayed him.

Careful attention to the casting and unique characterizations of all the roles will help ensure an effective production.

— *J. C.*

CONTENTS

ACT I 1

Scene 1 .... *1*
Late afternoon, the Inn 1
- SONG: "Wayside Inn" 1
- SONG: "The Rescue" 2
- DANCE: "The Entrance Polonaise" 4
- Song: "Friend #1" 8

Scene 2 .... *10*
Immediately following, the Lady's bedroom 10
- SONG: "Goodbye, My Sweet!" 10

Scene 3 .... *14*
Immediately following. The Inn 14
- SONG: "Romance" 15

Scene 4 .... *19*
Immediately following. The Garden. Moonlight 19
- SONG: "Lover Lost" 21

Scene 5 .... *24*
That evening, before dinner. The Inn 24
- SONG: "Once You've Had A Little Taste" 25
- SONG: "Friend #2" 28
- SONG: "Hulla Baloo Balay" 30
- SONG: REPRISE - "Once You've Had A Little Taste" 32
- DANCE: "The Dinner Minuet" 33

Scene 6 .... *34*
That evening after dinner. A hallway in the Inn 34

Scene 7 .... *35*
Immediately following. The Inn 35
- SONG: "You'd Be Amazed" 36
- SONG: "With A Friend Like You" 41
- "Wayside Inn" THEME 44
- SONG: "Come To The Masquerade" 45

Scene 8 47
  That night. The Garden 47
    SONG: "Man With A Load Of Mischief" 48
    SONG: REPRISE - "Come To The
    Masquerade" 50

ACT II 51

Scene 1 51
  The Inn. The next morning 51
    SONG: "What Style!" 51
    SONG: "A Wonder" 55
    SONG: "Make Way For My Lady" 57
    SONG: "Forget" 58
    SONG: "Any Other Way" 62
    SONG: "Little Rag Doll" 64

Scene 2 66
  The Garden, immediately following 66
    SONG: REPRISE— "Romance" 66
    SONG: "Sextet" 72
    SONG: REPRISE - "Make Way For My Lady" 74

ACT I
Scene 1

Late afternoon, the Inn

Music continues after Overture as the traveler opens on a small, countryside inn. The main entrance leads to the inn yard. There is a back entrance to the garden, a portion of which can be seen. There is a door to the kitchen, and stairs leading up to the bedrooms. A large fireplace is the principal feature of the inn. There are serving boards, tables, chairs. It is a plain room, but not drab—a cheerful note about it.

MUSIC In.

At the curtain it is dusk and the stage is rather dim. The INNKEEPER *is discovered at center door with lantern in hand.* HE'S *a small man, rather stout, good-natured, likes his drink.*

SONG: "Wayside Inn"
INNKEEPER. *(Sings)*
    AN OPEN DOOR
    AN EMPTY HOUSE
(INNKEEPER *steps in to hang lantern*)
    I'M WORKING FOR
    THE KITCHEN MOUSE
    MY COAT I'LL DOFF
    AND SETTLE BACK
    FOR WE ARE OFF
    THE BEATEN TRACK
(*Speaks*) We'll have no customers this night—unless it be a drunken farmer or a soldier out of service, and they need no glimmer to guide them while their noses show the way. (*Drops his coat on settle*) —Past eight o'clock! Heigho. A drop of comfort would not be amiss. (*Sings*)
    WHEN THINGS ARE CALM

> AT OUR WAYSIDE INN
> I GET ME BALM
> FROM A DROP OF GIN
> I GET ME BALM
> FROM A DROP OP GIN —

(Sits, chair right)
> GOD SAVE HONEST FOLK
> WHO OFTEN ROAM
> THE DEVIL TAKE TRAVELERS
> WHO STAY AT HOME

(WIFE *enters in a state of great agitation.* SHE *is a jolly woman but has more drive than her husband and is sharper tongued.* SHE *grabs his coat and puts it on him)*

WIFE. On with your coat and give the bottle here! Smartly there, smartly! For shame on you. With guests of quality on the road and expected any moment.
INNKEEPER. Guests? Quality? You've gone daft, woman.
WIFE. I'll give you daft. Get a move on! *(Takes lantern off hook)* There's work to do.

SONG: "The Rescue"
(Sings)
> OPEN THE SHUTTERS AND KINDLE THE FIRE
> GO TO THE CELLAR AND BRING UP THE WINE
> A CARRIAGE IS COMING WITH LADY AND MAID
> AND RIDING ALONG IS A LORD AND HIS MAN
> HURRY, HURRY, HURRY, HURRY
> DOWN WITH YOUR BOTTLE AND LOOK ALIVE
> WE HAVE A BUNDLE OF WORK TO DO!
> QUALITY'S COMING THIS VERY NIGHT

*(*SHE *takes lantern off)*

INNKEEPER. *(Unmoved)* What would such fine people be doing off the main highway? No, old Dutch, out there in the twilight, your eyes will play tricks on you.
WIFE. *(Returning)* It's a gentleman, I tell you, and a lady—

Act One Scene 1 3

and as fine a looking couple as I've ever set eyes on. It was the accident that brought them together. With my own eyes I saw the horses bolt and tear off down the hill. A runaway coach! It was very near a funeral, too—but for the lord and his man rescuing them in the nick of time. Oh, how I love an exciting rescue!!
(Sings)
    GALLOPING, GALLOPING RUNAWAY COACH
INNKEEPER. Aye, there will be accidents along the road, Wife. But that don't mean they'll be stopping here.
WIFE. You're hopeless. Absolutely hopeless! The coach would have to hit you before you'd stir a muscle.
INNKEEPER. And you'd have me work up a lather for no good reason.
WIFE. Hush, you pumpkin! I think I hear them. *(Goes to door,*

WIFE.	INNKEEPER.
(Sings)	*(Simultaneously)*
GO TO THE CELLAR AND BRING UP THE WINE	WHEN THINGS ARE CALM
A CARRIAGE IS COMING WITH LADY AND MAID	AT OUR WAYSIDE INN
AND RIDING ALONG IS A LORD AND HIS MAN	
HURRY, HURRY HURRY, HURRY	I GET ME BALM
DOWN WITH YOUR BOTTLE AND LOOK ALIVE	FROM A DROP OF GIN
WE HAVE A BUNDLE OF WORK TO DO	I GET ME BALM

center, looks out)

WIFE	INNKEEPER
(*Continued*)	(*Continued*)
QUALITY'S COMING	
THIS VERY NIGHT	FROM A DROP OF GIN
GALLOPING, GALLOPING	
RUNAWAY COACH	GOD SAVE HONEST
GALLOPING, GALLOPING	FOLK
LADY INSIDE	
GALLOPING, GALLOPING	
CAME THE MEN	
GALLOPING, GALLOPING	WHO OFTEN ROAM!
RIGHT BEHIND	
FASTER, FASTER	THE DEVIL TAKE
FASTER, FASTER	TRAVELERS
FINALLY ONE OF THEM	WHO STAY
CAUGHT THE REINS	
GALLOPING, GALLOPING	
PULLED THEM IN	
GALLOPING, GALLOPING	AT
SAVED THE DAY	
GALLOPING, GALLOPING	HOME
RUNAWAY COACH	
GALLOPING, GALLOPING	
GALLOPING, GALLOPING	
HOME!	

(*At the end, the Innkeeper turns away with a final big yawn and stretch, draining the last of his drink. Wife turns to the front entrance to greet the arrivals, curtsying deeply. MUSIC up strongly on a different theme*)

DANCE: "The Entrance Polonaise"

MAN *enters with trunk.* MAID *enters with bag.* LORD

Act One	Scene 1	5

> *enters.* LADY *enters.* THEY *do a turn around the room, during which the* INNKEEPER *goes up to center doors and closes them. All this is executed like a formal Polonaise. The* LORD *and* LADY *enter with a sweep, but with studied, dignified grace.* SHE *is a beautiful, proud woman;* HE *a dashing, handsome gentleman. The* MAID *is pretty but rather flighty, well aware of* HER *attractiveness. At the moment* SHE *is still near hysterics. The* MAN *is quiet, enigmatic. The* INNKEEPER *can hardly believe* HIS *eyes and can only stand there helplessly for awhile. The* WIFE *is too eager to please. The entrance builds to a climax as* THEY *assume formalized poses, then ends.*

MUSIC Out.
(The MAID *groans and almost faints into chair.* INNKEEPER *helps her to DR bench)*

WIFE. I hope your ladyship feels no ill effects from the shaking?
LADY. I thank you, no. It was a trifle, thanks to the happy arrival of this—these gentlemen.
WIFE. A trifle! My blood runs cold when I think of it. Why, there's the high cliff and the bend in the road— and the crazy horses tearing along, and —
LORD. I think we must allow that our arrival did come at a propitious moment.
WIFE. Yes. I do love bravery in a man— *(Curtsies to* LORD *and looks at the* MAN*)* —whoever he be!
LADY. I quite agree with you.
LORD. Still, madam, the virtue becomes a woman best.
LADY. The virtue, my lord, or virtue?
LORD. Courage is the only virtue, wise men tell us.
LADY. *(Laughing)* Then my maid is a sad rogue.
INNKEEPER. *(Coming out of his stupor, bows)* Good evening to your honor.
MAN. *(Correcting him)* Your lordship.

LORD. (*To his* MAN) Let him bring the best Madeira in his cellar.
INNKEEPER. A welcome to your lordship. You caught us a bit unawares, m'lord, but I'll do me best to —
LORD. Is this the innkeeper? (*Not looking at him*)
MAN. It is, my lord.
LORD. Then let him bring his wine. (*Stands*)
LADY. We must leave you to your Madeira, with our thanks once again. (*Curtsies*) You, my lord. (*To the* MAN) And you also, sir.
             MUSIC In.
(*The* MAN *bows.* WIFE *and* MAID *proceed upstairs carrying the* LADY'S *bag and trunk*)
WIFE. This way, my lady. Ours is only a wayside inn; but your ladyship will not look for a palace.
LADY. A palace? No, indeed. Your attic will be welcome. (THEY *exit upstairs. The* MAN *notices* INNKEEPER *still standing about, not wishing to miss any action.* MAN *makes an impatient gesture and* INNKEEPER *starts out to the kitchen*)
INNKEEPER. (Sings)
 HERE'S TO QUALITY WHO COME TO STAY
 SO GOD BLESS ACCIDENTS ALONG THE WAY
(*Exits*)
LORD. (*Sitting in chair, L.* MAN *takes off his spurs, then crosses right to saddlebags*) So, Charles, suddenly, at the fall of dusk, comes adventure, and Beauty smiles her thanks. Beauties— for they are happily plural. (INNKEEPER *enters from left with wine on a tray*) Adventure must be held in delicate fingers. (INNKEEPER *places wine glass between his outstretched fingers*) It should be sipped, not swallowed at a gulp. So here's a toast to prudence. Prudence, Charles! To that virtue I would empty a tumbler. (*Drinks and makes a face*)
INNKEEPER. I hope the Madeira is to your Lordship's taste?
LORD. (*To the* MAN) Is this the innkeeper?
MAN. It is, my Lord.

Act One   Scene 1   7

LORD. (*Not looking at him*) Your wine, like your person; is the soul of mediocrity. (*Puts glass on tray*)

INNKEEPER. (*Flattered*) Your Lordship is too kind. (*Starts out*)

LORD. Stay. My servant here is my companion. Use him well. He is the last survivor of his race—the breed of fools. Also he is my confessor, and lends me the comfort of philosophy.

INNKEEPER. Ha, ha! Your Lordship is pleased to make merry. But you will have pleasanter company this evening—a deal pleasanter, I'll be bound. Well, well, no harm in that, say I. There's a time for everything. (LORD *looks at him for the first time and not with pleasure*) I was young myself once, ha, ha! Youth will be served!

LORD. Charles!

MAN. My lord?

LORD. Remove this creature.

INNKEEPER. I meant no offense, my Lord. (*Exits, left. The* LORD *goes to* CHARLES, *becoming almost confidential*)

LORD. Charles, you are the most discreet manservant I have ever had, but you may be frank with me. Would you say my standing with the Prince is at the best?

MAN. (*Brushing* LORD'S *jacket*) No, my lord. I would say it was a bit precarious at the moment.

LORD. Precisely. I was too indiscreet with him at the gaming tables, and this time I am unable to cover my debt to him. It could go hard.

MAN. It could, my lord.

LORD. But you know who these adventurous ladies are. And you must have guessed that our meeting with them was not altogether by chance.

MAN. I think even your lordship did not foresee the accident to the coach.

LORD. No. That lent us the appearance of gallant rescuers. Let us make the most of it.

MAN. We will, my lord.

(*The* MAID *enters from upstairs with a pitcher. The* LORD *clears his throat and turns away*)
LORD. Charles, look to the horses. I want to know exactly how lame they are.
(*The* MAN *bows and exits right. The* MAID *goes up to the* LORD *by the fireplace.* HE *surveys her carefully, causing her to blush*)
MAID. Your pardon, sir—(*Curtsies*)—my lord, I mean. I must fetch warm water for my lady.
LORD. My lady can wait awhile. Set down the pitcher. (SHE *does so*) Come to me. (SHE *does so*) Give me your hand. (SHE *obeys, and* HE *puts money in it*) There, are we better friends?
MAID. (*Curtsies*) Much better, indeed, my lord. My lady —
LORD. Well, pretty one?
MAID. (*Pouting*) Why should I bother? I was almost killed because of her.
LORD. Do you not love your mistress?
MAID. I know my place, my lord.
LORD. But do you love her?
MAID. I hate her! I hate her, with her pride and her spirit and her smiling ways! (The LORD is amused) My lord will find my lady hard to please.
LORD. But some gentlemen no doubt have found her otherwise?
MAID. Perhaps. One here and there, my lord.
LORD. Gentlemen who—shall we say—had assistance. (*Sings*)

Song: "Friend #1"

WITH A FRIEND LIKE YOU —
MAID. What do you mean—"assistance?"
LORD. (*Sings*)
TO CONFIDE IN ME AND TRY TO SEE ME THROUGH—
(*Gives* HER *a coin.* SHE *smiles.*)
MAID. Well, I have done certain favors—but she is hard to

Act One Scene 1

    please.
LORD. (Sings)
    WITH A FRIEND THAT I COULD TRUST
    (*Gives* HER *another coin*)
MAID. Not too hard to please.
LORD. (*Sings*)
    I COULD DO THE THINGS I MUST —
    (*Another coin*)
MAID. For you—she'd be child's play.
LORD. (*Sings*)
    IF I JUST COULD HAVE A FRIEND
MAID. (Sings)
    SHE COULD EAS'LY BE A FRIEND
(*Simultaneously :*)

MAID.	LORD.
TO YOU	LIKE YOU

(*Blackout. Traveler closes 3/4. Bedroom wagon moves into place*)

Lights up on traveler.

Scene 2

Immediately following, the Lady's bedroom

LADY'S *trunk and carpet bag are open on wagon.* MAID *is discovered at open trunk.*

MUSIC Out.

LADY. (*Enters between traveler and wagon*) Thank you, Louise. You may go to your own room now.
MAID. Does not your ladyship want me to stay and help you change?
LADY. It will not be necessary, thank you.
MAID. (*Holds up trousers that were lying over the open trunk*) Surely you'll not be needing these, my lady. 'Tis a pair of breeches to an old costume.
LADY. (*Taking it back*) Believe me, Louise. I can manage.
MAID. (*Sulking,* SHE *backs out*) Sorry, mu'um.
LADY. I don't mean to be cross, Louise. It's been a trying day.
MAID. Trying for me also, my lady. Excuse me for saying so—but I don't think we should ever have left Bath. (*Exits*)
LADY. Foolish girl. I should never have brought her along. One travels faster alone.

MUSIC in.

(*Looks at locket around her neck*) And you had your eye on her, too, didn't you, my prince? I shouldn't be at all surprised if it didn't go farther than that. Oh, why do I still have you hanging around my neck. (*Takes off locket*) You'll get over it soon, Georgie Porgy. You never miss anyone very long. (*As* SHE *sings the song,* SHE *takes boy's outfit from trunk and dresses in it as* SHE *sings. At end of song* SHE *flings locket into wings, right, and goes off with carpetbag*)

SONG: "Goodbye, My Sweet!"

Act One   Scene 2   11

> (*Sings*)
> YOU WERE SUCH A LOVELY MAN
> EV'RY LITTLE THING YOU DID FOR ME
> SO THOUGHTFUL, SO SWEET
> WHY, YOU MADE MY LIFE COMPLETELY
>   FULFILLED
> NEARLY KILLED ME WITH KINDNESSES
> YOUR HIGHNESS IS THE NICEST MAN
> I'D EVER WANT TO MEET.
> GOODBYE, MY SWEET!
>
> AN AMUSING SORT OF MAN,
> ALWAYS READY TO REPEAT YOUR FAVORITE
> STORY, SUCH FUN
> EV'RY DAY WITH YOU WAS SUNNY AND GAY
> AND THEY SAY YOU WERE HUMOROUS
> THE RUMOR IS THAT SOMEONE ONCE
> HAD EVEN HEARD YOU LAUGH
> GOODBYE, MY SWEET!
>
> EVEN THOUGH YOU WERE SICKLY
> THOUGH YOUR GOUT MUST HAVE PAINED
> THERE WERE NIGHTS
> WHEN YOU HARDLY COMPLAINED
> YOU JUST KEPT IT TO YOURSELF
> WHILE YOU KEPT ME ON THE SHELF 'TIL YOU
> DESIRED ME AGAIN
> AND MY LIFE TO YOU WAS PLAINLY A TOY
> SUCH A JOY BRINGING CHEERS TO YOU
> WELL, HERE'S TO YOU, THE NICEST MAN
> I'D EVER WANT TO MEET—
> GOODBYE, MY SWEET!
>
> YES, I'M LEAVING YOU YOUR LITTLE WORLD
>   TO PLAY WITH
> SPEAKING PLAINLY, I HAVE HAD YOU UP TO
>   HERE

I REFUSE TO SPEND ANOTHER BLOODY DAY
    WITH
ANY MAN WHO CALLS ME NOTHING BUT "MY
    DEAR."
"MY DEAR," MY DEAR!
MY DEAR SWEET PRINCE
JUST THE SOUND OF "MY DEAR"
CAN MAKE ME WINCE
WHEN YOU'D SMILE THAT SMILE
AND DROP THOSE HINTS
IT WAS ALL I COULD DO TO FORCE MYSELF TO
    REMEMBER —
YOU'RE THE PRINCE

(*Spoken*) With any sort of luck I would have been in London tonight, and by tomorrow on a packet to Calais—safely out of your reach. But for those beautiful, high-strung steeds bolting at the sight of a fallen branch. Ah yes, the very horses you gave me for my birthday last.

(*Sings*)
YOU WERE GENEROUS AT HEART
AND YOU ALWAYS HAD ENOUGH OF YOUR
    AFFECTIONS TO SPARE
SO YOU SIMPLY CHOSE TO SHARE THEM
    AROUND
WHEN YOU FOUND ME SO PENNILESS
COULD ANY LESS A MAN HAVE HAD ME
CRAWLING AT HIS FEET?
AU REVOIR, MON PETIT!

I KNOW YOU'RE ON MY TRAIL
BUT DON'T THINK YOU'LL EVER FIND ME
    HERE
IN THIS PLACE, SO QUICK
I'LL BE GONE, YOU'LL NEVER PICK UP MY
    TRACK
I'LL GO BACK WHERE THE STAGE IS

EARN MY WAGES AND BE FREE OF
YOUR OUTRAGEOUS KIND OF LIFE!
GOODBYE MY SWEET
THOUGH YOUR COACH MAY RUN FASTER, D '
   YOU
THINK I'LL WAIT HERE, YOU BASTARD, YOU?
GOODBYE, GOODBYE, MY SWEET!

                               BLACKOUT

                     HARPSICHORD MUSIC

(*Bedroom wagon off. Traveler closes*)

Scene 3

Immediately following. The Inn

Lights on traveler. The WIFE *is discovered sewing, right. The* INNKEEPER *enters left. The* LORD *and the* MAID. *appear during the song.*

INNKEEPER. Which rooms did you make ready?
WIFE. The two best bedrooms on the first landing.
INNKEEPER. Hum! I would have put them further apart. This is what the quality call a romance.
WIFE. And why not? We have no call to meddle with the pleasures of the quality.
INNKEEPER. That's as may be, but I would have bedded them further apart.
(*Traveler opens*)
             MUSIC Out.
            (HARPSICHORD)
WIFE. Tsch!
INNKEEPER. These romances are here today and gone tomorrow.
WIFE. That's not the way of true love.
              MUSIC In.
INNKEEPER. (*Sings*)
  TRUE LOVE! TRUE LOVE! TRUE LOVE!
  WHAT DO THEY KNOW ABOUT TRUE LOVE?
  CERTAINLY NO MORE THAN ME OR YOU, LOVE
  THOUGH THIS GENTLEMAN AND LADY HAVE
    MANNERS THAT ARE SPLENDID,
  BED THEM CLOSE TOGETHER, AND SOON
    THEIR STAY IS ENDED—
  NOW, SERVANTS AND MAIDS—
  WELL, THEY'RE MORE LIKE US!
  THEY DON'T PLAY CHARADES,
  THEY DON'T MAKE NO FUSS
  SO KEEP THE UPPER CLASSES PACIFIED
  BUT BED THE COMMON PEOPLE SIDE BY SIDE!

Act One   Scene 3   15

WIFE. (*Speaks*) Indeed I will not! I'll have no goings-on in this house.
INNKEEPER. (*Sings*)
>GOINGS-ON! GOINGS-ON! GOINGS-ON!
>TRUE LOVE! TRUE LOVE! TRUE LOVE!
>IF A POOR MAN HAS A FLING, IT'S JUST AN ANTIC
>IF HE'S RICHER THAN A KING, THEN IT'S ROMANTIC!

SONG: "Romance"

(INNKEEPER)
>A YOUNG LADY'S ROOM IS A STEP DOWN THE HALL
>AND THINGS START TO HAPPEN IN NO TIME AT ALL
>NOW, IF YOU ARE POOR THAT' S A COMMON ADVANCE
>BUT IF YOU ARE RICH, IT'S ROMANCE!

WIFE.
>ROMANCE!

INNKEEPER.
>ROMANCE!

WIFE.
>ROMANCE!

INNKEEPER.
>A DASHING AND SMASHING ROMANCE!

(*Music under*)
WIFE. (*Speaks*) Oh, no. With the quality it ain't like that.
INNKEEPER. (*Speaks*) It ain't, eh? (*Sings*)
>NOW YOU KNOW AND I KNOW THE WAYS OF TRUE LOVE
>BUT ASK THAT YOUNG NOBLE WHAT HE' S THINKING OF:
>I BET IF HE COULD, AND YOU GAVE HIM THE CHANCE,
>HE'D TELL YOU HE'S PLANNING —

LORD.
—ROMANCE

ALL.
ROMANCE!
ROMANCE!
ROMANCE!
A FRANTIC, ROMANTIC—ROMANCE!
EV'RYBODY'S GOT A DIFF'RENT VIEW
LOVE AFFAIRS ARE VERY DIFF'RENT, TOO!

INNKEEPER.
BASICALLY WE'RE REALLY ALL THE SAME—
IT'S MERELY A QUESTION OF WHAT'S IN A NAME!

WIFE.
WHEN I WAS A GIRL I HAD ONLY ONE PLAN
TO MARRY A HANDSOME, ROMANTIC YOUNG MAN
I MUST HAVE BEEN DAFT OR IN SOME SORT OF TRANCE
MY PLANS GOT MISCARRIED,
INDEED I GOT MARRIED,
BUT WHERE, FOR GOD'S SAKE, IS ROMANCE?

ALL.
ROMANCE! ROMANCE!

LORD.
THESE DAYS AN AFFAIR IS SO OFTEN A WASTE
UNLESS THE AFFAIR CAN BE DONE WITH GREAT TASTE
I'LL BE VERY CAREFUL, LEAVE NOTHING TO CHANCE AND MAKE IT A WORTHWHILE ROMANCE

ALL.
ROMANCE!
ROMANCE!
ROMANCE!

LORD.
ECSTATIC, EMPHATIC ROMANCE!

Act One Scene 3

MAID.
>I STIFLE A LAUGH WHEN I HEAR MEN PROCLAIM
>THEIR TRUE LOVE FOR ME WILL BE ALWAYS THE SAME
>NEXT MORNING THEY LEAVE ME WITH HARDLY A GLANCE
>OH, AIN'T IT A KICK IN THE PANTS!

ALL.
>THE PANTS!
>THE PANTS!
>THE PANTS!

MAID.
>THAT'S NOT WHAT I'D CALL A ROMANCE!

WIFE.
>IT'S EXOTIC.

INNKEEPER.
>IT'S EROTIC.

MAID.
>IT' S HYPNOTIC.

LORD.
>PATRIOTIC.

ALL.
>HOW CHAOTIC!
>IT'S MERELY A QUESTION OF WHAT'S IN A NAME.
>NOW, SOME SAY IT'S TEARFUL AND SOME SAY IT'S GAY,
>AND SOME FIND A YEARFUL AND SOME JUST A DAY
>BUT THERE IS ONE FACT THAT WE ALL OF US FACE:
>THERE'S NOTHING THAT'S TAKING ITS PLACE!
>ROMANCE!
>ROMANCE!
>ROMANCE!
>THERE'S NOTHING THAT'S TAKING ITS PLACE

(*Coda:*)
>ONE CANNOT OPPOSE IT
>AND EV'RYONE KNOWS IT
>SO HIGHLY WE SPEAK OF
>A NIGHT OR A WEEK OF

WIFE.
>EXCITING, INVITING

INNKEEPER.
>OH, RIPPING AND GRIPPING

LORD.
>TERRIFIC, SPECIFIC

ALL.
>A SOARING AND ROARING
>IT NEVER IS BORING ROMANCE!

(MAID, INNKEEPER, WIFE *exit left;* LORD *exits right.* BLACKOUT *into blue on Traveler*)

ALL. (*Sung offstage*)
>ROMANCE!
>ROMANCE!
>ROMANCE!
>AHH-H-H-H-H-H-H!!!

(*On third beat, open traveler*)

Scene 4

Immediately following. The Garden. Moonlight

The garden is in the full bloom of late summer. It is not a formal, landscaped garden, but quite pretty as simple country gardens often are. The LADY *enters disguised as a boy, and* SHE *carries a small bag. As* SHE *starts to run out the* MAN *enters with a lantern which* HE *holds aloft.* SHE *breaks away down right.*

MAN. Who is that?
LADY. Stable boy, your worship.
                                                    MUSIC Out.
(SHE *breaks down left*)
MAN. Hold there! If you're the stable boy, what are you doing about in the garden?
LADY. Always had a feeling for roses, I have.
MAN. I see you have a feeling for lying, too. (HE *snatches cap from her head and her hair tumbles down*) My lady!
LADY. (*She returns stare, and there is a pause*) Many's the time I've played young boys on the stage, but it appears my old skills have escaped me. (SHE *moves away from him, trying to hide her nervousness*) While we are alone, I have to thank you once again for this evening's service. You are a gallant man.
MAN. Your ladyship honors me.
LADY. If the question is not impertinent, why did you choose this trade of all trades?
MAN. It is a trade like any other.
LADY. You see the world, it is true.
MAN. I have eyes and ears, my lady. (*Reaches for her bag*) Shall I carry that for you?
LADY. But I'm not going inside.
MAN. My lady —

LADY. I am in a trap, it seems. Too many persons have an interest in this journey of mine, and I do not choose to submit to their attentions. Will you help me escape?
MAN. My lady's horses are lame.
LADY. I can ride, if need be.
MAN. We have no mounts ourselves.
LADY. I can walk to the next inn.
MAN. Twelve miles, my lady. The night is dark—and there are highwaymen in these parts.
LADY. So you are not disposed to help me? I was mistaken in you. (*Starts off*)
MAN. If my lady fears that she may be followed from Bath, I can tell her that the danger is past.
LORD. (*With spirit*) You can tell me?
MAN. The Prince's coach has been directed by the high road to Oxford.
LADY. Misdirected?
MAN. As my lady pleases.
LADY. Who has done this? Who are you, sir?
MAN. I am a friend.
LADY. If you will pardon me for saying so, I have heard that approach before. However, I must take it on trust, for plainly you know me.
MAN. I know you better than I know myself.
LADY. (*Laughs*) Here are deep waters indeed. (*Goes to him*) I do not remember your face.
MAN. It is five years since my lady was a singer at Drury Lane.
LADY. And you were —
MAN. I was one of many admirers.
LADY. (*Smiles*) Only five years, can it be? It seems half a lifetime. I have traveled far since then. The music has run out of my horses' hoofs.
MAN. My lady was well loved.
LADY. Was I? I didn't find that. (*Pause*) What is this place?
MAN. It is a simple alehouse called "The Man with a Load of Mischief."
LADY. Another man! God save us, I am weary of them. —So

Act One   Scene 4

the Prince takes the wrong turning—outriders, coach and all?
MAN. He will pass in the night.
LADY. Outriders, coach and all. There's a chapter ended. Put not your trust in Princes. (*Pauses*) You know that I was his mistress?
MAN. So much every one knows.
LADY. Ask me why I chose that trade of all trades.
MAN. My lady has seen the world.
LADY. A sort of world. A world seen through a myriad of lovers. Too many fops. Too few men. Too many wits and too little honesty. Lackeys.
MAN. My lady speaks to a lackey.
LADY. No. I think that you and I are in league against our betters.
MAN. My lady must speak for herself.
LADY. You did not call his lordship when you discovered me leaving just now.
MAN. I could still do so.
LADY. But I don't think you will. Believe me, my friend—I trust you.
MAN. Good servants are made to be trusted. (*A short pause*) I must escort you in now, my Lady.
LADY. Must?
MAN. His Lordship anticipates your presence at dinner. If you were not there—
LADY. Then, as you say, I must. (HE *picks up her bag* THEY *exit into the Inn,* HE *taking the lantern with* HIM.)

(The garden becomes darker. Lady puts on a full length cloak.)

SONG: "Lover Lost"

LADY. (*Sings*)
    I RUN A RACE WITH MY PAST
    I RUN FROM LOVES THAT NEVER LAST
    IF I SHOULD LOSE, THEN WHO'S TO BLAME?

SO MANY LOVERS, YET ALL THE SAME.

    LOVER STRONG
    LOVER BRITTLE
    ASKING MUCH
    GIVING LITTLE
    LOVER CURT
    SEEMING KINDLY
    LOVER HURT
    ACTING BLINDLY

(LORD *enters.*)
    LOVERS BEYOND RECALL
    LOVERS, I'VE KNOWN YOU ALL —

(*Music continues. The* LADY *turns slightly startled, as* SHE *sees the* LORD.)
(*Speaks*) Oh! You startled me, my lord.
(SHE *stays in the shadows. Cloak hides boy's costume*)
                                            MUSIC Out.

LORD. Forgive me. But seeing you here in the moonlight — it was such a lovely vision, I disliked disturbing you. (Looks around) I thought I noticed) — (Pause)
LADY. Yes, my lord?
LORD. It seemed to me I saw the golden light of a lantern. I find it is only your beauty lighting up the night.
LADY. You are too kind, my lord.
                                             MUSIC In.
LORD. Is it not time we dress for dinner?
LADY. Shortly, my lord. Shortly.
LORD. So, you will sup with me. This is an honor indeed.
LADY. Call it rather the payment of a debt.
LORD. To a man whose debts are unpaid, your integrity is overwhelming.
LADY. Always excepting debts of honor?
LORD. (*Approaches her*) We pay those from necessity. I am looking forward to our dining together. It seems we are the only guests in this poor in. A crude setting perhaps, but it will give me the opportunity of saying to you — all the things I have been wanting to say.

Act One   Scene 4   23

LADY. *(Drops her head)* My lord.
LORD. May I escort you in, my dear?
LADY. If you do not mind, sir, I will remain in the garden a moment longer. I like the night air.
LORD. It becomes you royally, madam. *(*HE *makes a move to put his arm around* HER. SHE *moves easily away, sniffs the air.* HE *bows)* By your leave, then. Until dinner.
*(*HE *exits into inn.)*
LADY. *(Sings)*
    LOVERS, I'VE KNOWN YOU ALL
    LOVER CALM
    LOVER NERVOUS
    MY HEART WAS EVER
    AT THEIR SERVICE
    NOW I LAUGH
    AND WONDER WHY —
    FOR NEVER ONCE
    IN LOVE WAS I.

BLACKOUT

(Traveler closes. Blue wash on Traveler)

Scene 5

That evening, before dinner. The Inn

(*Different music theme up. Ambers up on traveler. The* LORD *enters from right, the* MAID *from left*)

LORD. (*Arching his brow*) More warm water for my lady?
MAID. (*Pertly*) The first grew cold—waiting for her.
LORD. I see— (*Suddenly very firm and cold*) Tell me, have we not all met before today? At Bath, I think? Was it not in the best house of all—from which my lady has just run away as fast as her coach would carry her?
MAID. (*Startled*) You know too much, my lord!
LORD. I have eyes in my head.
              MUSIC Out.
MAID. (*Thoroughly frightened; starts out*) I must go to my lady.
LORD. (*Stops her, laughing*) Come, it is no hanging matter to run away from a man. The woman who runs will never lack followers.
MAID. If my lady could hear you, she would fly into a rage!
LORD. A woman of spirit, eh? I see. But you have no intention of telling her, do you? (*Puts his arm around her and whispers in her ear*)
MAID. (*Pulls away, but just a bit*) Oh fie, my lord! I know my place.
LORD. Good. It is the art of life to know it—I think you can keep a secret.
MAID. Oh?
LORD. Yes. After all, you told me you hated her.
MAID. Oh, her! But for you, my lord, we should both have been lying in a ditch with the coach atop of us. And all because she fell out with her Prince. A lover's quarrel, and she thought herself insulted. A Prince, too.
 (*Traveler opens.* THEY *move into set.* MUSIC *to cover*

Act One Scene 5 25

traveler)
LORD. *The* Prince, my girl. A world of difference.
MAID. As open-handed a gentleman as ever stepped.
LORD. You should be a lady-in-waiting, if we all had our rights.
MAID. Oh, my lord, you understand indeed! She never would! To flounce out of the house without so much as a farewell, and half our baggage left behind—to sit cramped in a coach—Oh, it was such a fine life at Bath—

MUSIC In.
—beautiful clothes and strolls along the river, and the Italian singers at the playhouse, and a servant's ball every week.

(*The "Romance" theme. Sings*)
    MUSIC IN THE GARDENS EV'RY NIGHT
    PARTIES IN THE PALACE LEFT AND RIGHT
    FANCY DINNERS WHEN YOU SIT TO SUP
    NOW, WHO'D BE A FOOL AN' GIVE ALL O' THAT
        UP?

SONG: "Once You've Had A Little Taste"

MAID. (*Continued*)
    OH, ONCE YOU'VE HAD A LITTLE TASTE OF
        PINK CHAMPAGNE
    IT'S HARD TO SETTLE BACK AND DRINK YOUR
        BEER
    ONCE YOU'VE SPENT A DAY OR TWO IN
        LONDON TOWN
    YOU WISH THAT YOU COULD STAY THERE FOR
        A YEAR
    ONCE YOU'VE HAD A LITTLE BITE OF CAVIAR,
        IT'S DIFFICULT TO SWALLOW CHIPS
        AND STOUT
    AND ONCE YOU'VE HAD A TASTE OF ALL THAT
        HIGH, HIGH LIVIN'

IT CERTAINLY IS HARD TO DO WITHOUT.
ONCE I HAD A LITTLE ROOM THAT I CALLED HOME
AND RIGHT WITHIN A PRINCE'S PALACE WALL
TWICE I VERY NEARLY HAD THE PRINCE HIMSELF
PICK UP MY HANKY WHEN I LET IT FALL
HENCE A GENTLEMAN APPEARED AND FANCIED ME
I PROVED TO HIM THAT I WAS JUST HIS KIND
OH, ONCE YOU'VE BEEN IN FRONT OF ALL THAT HIGH, HIGH LIVIN'
IT'S QUITE A CHORE TO LEAVE IT ALL BEHIND.
ONCE THE HIGH LIFE YOU HAVE TASTED
YOU FEEL LIKE YOUR TOTAL LIFE'S BEEN WASTED
ONCE YA DANCE 'EM—ONCE YA KISSED 'EM
YOU CAN'T GET IT OUT OF YOUR BLOOMIN' SYSTEM
IF YOU'VE EVER SET A FIRE TO *CREPES SUZETTE*
IT'S HARD TO LIGHT THE STOVE AND WARM YOUR HASH
IF YOU'VE EVER HAD A GOWN OF FINEST SILK
IT'S HARD TO TAKE IT OFF AND SWEEP THE TRASH
IF YOU'VE EVER HAD A KISS FROM ROYALTY
IT'S HARD TO BE A BLOODY BUTCHER'S WIFE
'CAUSE ONCE YOU'VE HAD A TASTE OF ALL THAT HIGH, HIGH LIVIN'
YOU WISH THAT YOU COULD TASTE IT ALL YOUR LIFE.

(SHE dances)

IF YOU'VE EVER HAD A KISS FROM ROYALTY
IT'S HARD TO BE A BLOODY BUTCHER'S WIFE
OH! ONCE YOU'VE HAD A TASTE OF ALL THAT HIGH, HIGH LIVIN
YOU WISH THAT YOU COULD TASTE IT
(OH, CAN'T YOU ALMOST TASTE IT?)

YOU WISH THAT YOU COULD TASTE IT ALL
   YOUR LIFE.
YOU CAN TRY 'TO FORGET
BUT WHEN ONCE YOUR LIPS WERE WET
WITH PINK CHAMPAGNE, CREPES SUZETTE
A GENTLEMAN'S KISS, YOU'LL SURELY MISS
THE HIGH LIFE.
ONCE YOU HAVE A LITTLE TASTE!
                                         MUSIC Out.

(*At the end of her number, the* LORD *catches* HER *up in* HIS *arms and kisses* HER *again, this time more passionately. The* MAN *enters on this piece of business*)

LORD. Well, Charles? Fresh from the stable?
MAN. The mare has a saddle-gall, my lord.
LORD. Careless creature. (*To* MAID.) You and I will meet again. (*To* MAN) And your own mount? (MAID exits with pitcher)
MAN. A jar and some bruises. Scarcely fit to ride.
LORD. The coach horses are lame, no doubt?
MAN. Dead lame, my lord.
LORD. Then we are tethered here for some days. We have time to think. Now, this lady's coach may have other pursuers—who must be misdirected. You will post one or two stout fellows for the job. Bribe them handsomely. (*Throws purse to Man*) See to it now, and return.
MAN. I took the liberty an hour ago of carrying out your lordship's wishes.
LORD. (*Truly surprised*) The devil you did!
MAN. I posted a man to direct the Prince's coach to follow the highroad to Oxford.
LORD. Well done! You are a treasure, Charles. I could almost call you my better self. (*Pause*) We must still decide what to do with her ladyship. This woman interests me. A gilded plaything, a pretty parasite, a Prince's mistress. Well, you shall see her humbled. You shall

even assist at the ceremony.

MAN. I, my lord?

LORD. I have half a mind to send her back to her Prince.

MAN. (*Involuntarily*) That would be—

LORD. Magnificent, would it not? A noble gesture. He won a great deal from me last night at the tables. Well, the money is lost, but one can still be generous.

MAN. And if the lady will not go?

LORD. There are ways and means of persuading her. And you, my Charles, shall be her escort. That will lend irony to the stroke—I have no great love for these women who slip the collar. Too many of them would endanger the state—I can rely upon you?

MAN. (*slight pause*) As on your lordship's better self.

LORD. Then I will make ready for supper. (*Starts out*) We must preserve the semblance of gallantry with our runaways. They also have their pride, no doubt.

MAN. As much, my lord, as we shall leave them.

LORD. (*On the stairs*) Ha! As much as we shall leave them. Yes. Excellent fellow. Excellent fellow!

MUSIC In.

SONG: "Friend #2"

(*Sings*)
> WITH A FRIEND LIKE YOU
> TO CONFIDE IN ME AND TRY—

(*Speaks*) But it seems to me that you had your own reasons for misdirecting the coach.

MAN. My lord!

LORD. (*Sings*)
> OH, YOUR VIRTUE YOU'VE DISPLAYED
> BUT YOUR EYE'S BEEN ON THE MAID

MAN.
> BUT, MY LORD—

LORD.
> COME, NOW, CONFESS—

MAN.
> MY LORD—

LORD.
   IT'S TRUE!

MUSIC Out.

(*The* MAID *enters down the stairs as the* LORD *goes up and out.* HE *is laughing heartily, stops to pinch* HER *cheek, then exits. The* MAN *sits on bench center to work on a piece of harness. The* MAID *comes in the room—looks at* HIM *a long moment*)

MAID. Not so much as a look. Fine manners indeed!
MAN. Forgive me. My thoughts had gone wool gathering.
MAID. You and your gentlemanly airs. I know your sort.
MAN. And what is that?
MAID. You quiet ones. A girl never knows what you're thinking.
MAN. You prefer his lordship, I notice.
MAID. Oh, for shame! You were listening!
MAN. There was no need to listen.
MAID. (*Flirting*) But what if I gave his lordship the go-by? What if you should please me better?
MAN. I do not please women.
MAID. So you think maybe. But ask the women first.
MAN. Does not his lordship please you? (SHE *only shrugs at this*)
   Why, then, do you bother with him?
MAID. A girl has to get along. He has money, that I know.
MAN. Is that so important?
MAID. Listen, I knew a girl once. She was ever so sweet, she was. And pretty, too. You'd never find a prettier one. But she didn't have a thing in her life. Not a farthing! Huh! The only thing she ever had was a dirty rag doll when she was little. But when she grew up she learned to use her good looks—and her head. She's going to marry a real nobleman now— (*Gets carried away with her story*) —and have everything she wants in life—

MUSIC IN.

SONG: "Hulla Baloo Balay"

MAN. (*Sings*)
    FULL O' THE GLOW OF EARLY MAY—
MAID. Servants and carriages —
MAN.
    HULLABALOO BALAY—
MAID. And a house in the country—
MAN.
    WINTER IS SO FAR AWAY—
MAID. Happiness, that's what.
MAN.
    HULLABALOO BALAY.
    OH, ONCE THERE WAS A BRAVE, YOUNG LAD
    WITH HOPEFUL, SPARKLING EYES
    WHO SET UPON THE ROAD OF LIFE
    AND SHOUTED HIS GOODBYES.
    HE LONGED TO BE A CAPTAIN'S MATE
    AND SAIL THE SEA IN SHIPS
    HE STARTED OFF WITH CONFIDENCE
    A SONG WAS ON HIS LIPS
    FULL O' THE GLOW OF EARLY MAY
    HULLABALOO BALAY
    WINTER IS SO FAR AWAY
    HULLABALOO BALAY

    HIS BEATING HEART WAS FILLED WITH JOY
    A SPLENDID LIFE HE'D FORGE
    INSPIRED BY THE SPIRIT OF
    FAIR ENGLAND AND ST. GEORGE
    HE KEPT TO HIS DETERMINED PLAN
    A SONG STILL ON HIS LIPS
    AND SOON BECAME A CAPTAIN'S MATE
    AND SAILED THE SEA IN SHIPS
    FULL O' THE GLOW OF EARLY MAY
    HULLABALOO BALAY
    WINTER IS SO FAR AWAY
    HULLABALOO BALAY

Act One   Scene 5   31

        BUT, THEN ONE LONELY, MISTY NIGHT
        WHILE IN A DISTANT LAND
        HE WANDERED FAR AWAY FROM SHIPS
        AND FOUND A GYPSY BAND
        THEY TOOK HIM IN AND GAVE HIM WINE
        THAT SINGING, DANCING SWARM
        AND LATE THAT NIGHT THERE CAME TO HIM
        A MAIDEN SOFT AND WARM
(*Slower*)
        FULL O' THE GLOW OF EARLY MAY
        HULLABALOO BALAY
        WINTER IS SO FAR AWAY
(*Up tempo*)
        HULLABALOO BALAY
        THE NIGHT WAS FULL OF MUSIC
        FROM THE VERY HEART OF SPRING
        SHE FASTENED TO HIS BURNING EAR
        A GOLDEN GYPSY RING
        HE SOON FORGOT HIS SAILING SHIPS
        HE SOON FORGOT HIS DREAM
        HE SOON FORGOT THAT GYPSY MAIDS
        ARE SELDOM WHAT THEY SEEM
        FULL O' THE GLOW OF EARLY MAY
        HULLABALOO BALAY
        WINTER IS SO FAR AWAY
        HULLABALOO BALAY
        (SLOW)
        NEXT MORN HE WAS AWAKENED BY
        THE COLD AND MISTY DAWN
        AND WHEN HE LOOKED ABOUT THE PLACE
        THE CARAVAN WAS GONE
        AND NOW NO SONG IS ON HIS LIPS
        BUT STILL SOME DREAMS HAVE STAYED
        NOW, TELL ME, DOES HE DREAM OF SHIPS
        OR OF THAT GYPSY MAID?
(He *kisses* Her *hand*)

>   SOON THE GLOW IS GONE FROM MAY
>   HULLABALOO BALAY
>   WINTER'S NOT SO FAR AWAY
>   HULLABALOO BALAY

MAID. My hand was never kissed before.
MAN. It should have been.
MAID. Oh, I like you, man.
MAN. It is good of you to tell me that.
(*Sings*)
>   SOON THE GLOW IS GONE FROM MAY
>   HULLABALOO BALAY
>   WINTER'S NOT SO FAR AWAY
>   HULLABALOO BALAY

(*The* MAN *exits on this late note. The lights fade with the music, as the* MAID *watches after* HIM. *When the lights come back up, the* MAID *is still lost in thought and the* INNKEEPER *and his* WIFE *are entering*)

>   MUSIC out.

WIFE. There she is! Get a move on, girl. And do be careful there!
MAID. I'll be as careful as I need to be, thank you. I'll not let your grouching put me out of sorts. Not with a fancy dinner coming up.
INNKEEPER. Oh, the wife and I have been in service. We know how the quality like to dine, don't we, pet?
WIFE. 'Deed we do!
MAID. If you've served the quality, then you've had a taste of the high life yourself, I'll warrant. You might as well enjoy it.
INNKEEPER. That's telling her, girl!
WIFE. That's telling me, is it? I may not be the stick-in-the-mud you take me for. I remember what it was like.

>   MUSIC in.

SONG: REPRISE - "Once You've Had A Little Taste"

(WIFE sings)
>   ONCE YOU'VE HAD A LITTLE TASTE OF PINK

                    CHAMPAGNE
          IT'S HARD TO SETTLE BACK AND DRINK YOUR
                    BEER
Maid and Innkeeper.
          DRINK YOUR BEER!
Maid.
          ONCE YOU'VE SPENT A DAY OR TWO IN
                    LONDON TOWN
Maid and Wife.
          YOU WISH THAT YOU COULD STAY THERE FOR
                    A YEAR!
Innkeeper.
          FOR A YEAR!
All.
          ONCE YOU'VE HAD A LITTLE BITE OF CAVIAR
Innkeeper.
          IT'S DIFFICULT TO SWALLOW CHIPS AND
                    STOUT
All.
          ONCE YOU'VE HAD A TASTE OF ALL THAT
                    HIGH, HIGH LIVIN'—

(*The* Man *enters down stairs. The* Others *all stop short. Lights dim. Music changes to minuet.*)

DANCE: "The Dinner Minuet"

They *prepare the room for dinner,* Their *steps and movements all choreographed in the style of a formal minuet. On the sixth set of eight the* Lord *and then the* Lady *enter.* He *escorts* Her *to her seat and* They *sit. On the eighth set of eight the* Man *takes a rose from the bowl of roses* He *has brought on, and hands it to the* Lady. She *takes it, sniffs it; looks up at* Man. *Tableau*)

                                        MUSIC out.

DIM-OUT

Scene 6

That evening after dinner. A hallway in the Inn

Lights up on traveler. The WIFE *and Innkeeper enter from right.* SHE *is still glowing from the memory of the dinner.* HE *is picking* HIS *teeth.*

WIFE. Oh! That was a beautiful dinner!
INNKEEPER. Aye, that it was.
WIFE. And so romantic!
INNKEEPER. Aye, that it was.
WIFE. And such a handsome couple.
INNKEEPER. Aye, that they are.
WIFE. (*Sighs*) Well—here we are.
                MUSIC out.
INNKEEPER. (*A pause.* HE *eyes, a smile slowly spreading across* HIS *face*) Come along, Old Dutch. I feel the bite, too.

BLACKOUT

                 MUSIC in.

(INNKEEPER and WIFE exit left)

Scene 7

Immediately following. The Inn

Traveler opens. Lights up. Music out. The inn, right after the dinner. The Lord and the Lady are still at table. The Man and the Maid are in position. The Man is serving dessert.

LORD. Yet, madam, there is this to be said—(*Notices his dessert*)
 What have we here?
MAN. A dish of early strawberries, my lord.
LORD. Innocent fruit! They shall be dipped in wine. Madam?
LADY. (*To the Man*) I will take cream, if you please.
LORD. Berries and cream—a marriage of the innocents. Indeed a massacre, to any palate of distinction.
(*Pause*)
LADY. You may go, Louise. (MAID *bows and exits left, flirting with* LORD *as* SHE *goes. The* LORD'S *attention remains fixed on* HER. *Pause*) I think when we were interrupted, you were singing the praises of the dice.
LORD. Ah, yes, my dear. There is this to be said for the passion of gaming, that it improves the loser's character out of knowledge. A man never feels so virtuous as the morning after he has lost his money at the tables. All manner of fine thoughts and noble sentiments come into his mind. I have known men resolve to give up the dice forever, and at least one who held to the resolution for a week.
LADY. He was a hero indeed.
LORD. I have even known men determine to end their lives forthwith at pistol's point, which was the best service they could render to their fellows. Some actually did so. Their souls rest in the gamesters' paradise. (*Dabs at his mouth with his napkin*) To leave the world gracefully requires breeding.

35

MUSIC In.
LADY. Really?

SONG: "You'd Be Amazed"

LORD.
> I'M SURE YOU AGREE
> FOR YOU'RE SO LIKE ME
> SO MANY I COULD MENTION
> HAVEN'T HALF YOUR COMPREHENSION
> YES, YOU'RE LIKE ME
> BUT YOU'D BE AMAZED
> HOW SHALLOW SOME PEOPLE CAN BE

LADY.
> OH, I AGREE I AGREE
> YOU'LL NEVER KNOW HOW I AGREE
> AH YES, AH YES
> YOU SEE EVERYTHING JUST LIKE ME

BOTH.
> BUT YOU'D BE AMAZED
> HOW SHALLOW SOME PEOPLE CAN BE

(*Music continues under*)

LORD. (Speaks) Madam, I am overjoyed with your understanding. I find you are a woman of sense. A rare commodity.

LADY. You give me too much credit, my lord. I think you will find I am mere woman. I bow to my emotions rather than follow what reason tells me.

LORD. Reason?! Fah! There is nothing more over-rated than reason. Men reason to strengthen their own prejudices—not to disturb their adversary's convictions. There are many foolish fellows around today who wish to do away with dueling. They would have us solve our differences by reason! Dueling is the only civilized way of settling a gentleman's quarrel.

LADY. I have been the object of duels, my lord. The prize of death.

LORD. Such a prize might well be worth many an honorable

Act One Scene 7

death. Am I not right, Charles?
MAN. Quite so, my lord.
LORD. (*Sings*)
    I'M SURE YOU AGREE
    FOR YOU'RE SO LIKE ME
    I KNOW YOU UNDERSTAND ME
    THE SIMPLE TRUST YOU HAND ME
    YES, YOU'RE LIKE ME

(*Simultaneously:*)

LORD.	MAN.
I'M SURE YOU AGREE	I'M SURE
FOR YOU'RE SO LIKE ME	MY LORD
I KNOW YOU UNDERSTAND ME	OH YES, I AGREE
	I CERTAINLY DO
THE SIMPLE TRUST YOU HAND ME	THOUGH DIFF'RENT FROM YOU
YES, YOU'RE LIKE ME	YOU SEE CERTAIN THINGS JUST LIKE ME
BUT YOU'D BE AMAZED	BUT YOU'D BE AMAZED
HOW SHALLOW SOME PEOPLE CAN BE	HOW SHALLOW THEY CAN BE

(*Music continues under*)
LORD. If I did not know better, Charles, I would almost think we were of one mind.
LADY. Would that be so very odd, my lord?
LORD. Madam, my man has never yet agreed with me. On the day when we cease to fall out I shall dismiss him. He satisfies a craving inbred in us, the wrestler's instinct. A heart of oak, a spirit of steel.
LADY. We learn more of men every day. I blush to confess that my maid agrees with me on all occasions.
LORD. It is no more than her duty, my dear. Women —
LADY. Women are not wrestlers.
LORD. Wrestlers? Perish the thought! (*Becoming intimate*) Women are the most divine of God's creatures.

LADY. Oh, my lords and masters! Your world of compliments, your world of artifice, your world of sense and instinct.
LORD. It is the world we know, madam. The rest is guesswork. (*Sings*)
    I'M SURE YOU AGREE
    FOR YOU'RE SO LIKE ME
    ALL OTHERS FALL BEHIND YOU
    THE ANGELS HAVE DESIGNED YOU
    YES, YOU'RE LIKE ME

(*Simultaneously:*)

LORD.	LADY.	MAN.
I'M SURE YOU AGREE	OH, I AGREE, I AGREE	I'M SURE MY LORD
	YOU'LL NEVER KNOW	OH, YES, I AGREE
FOR YOU'RE SO LIKE ME	HOW I AGREE	I CERTAINLY DO
ALL OTHERS FALL BEHIND YOU	AH YES,	
		THOUGH DIFF'RENT FROM YOU
THE ANGELS HAVE DESIGNED YOU	AH YES YOU SEE EVERY-THING	YOU SEE CERTAIN THINGS
YES, YOU'RE LIKE ME	JUST LIKE ME	JUST LIKE ME

LORD.
    BUT YOU'D BE AMAZED HOW—
LADY.
    TIRESOME
LORD.
    HOW—
LADY.
    LOATHSOME
LORD.
    HOW—

Act One   Scene 7

LADY AND MAN.
    SHALLOW SOME PEOPLE CAN BE
LORD. Precisely!
(*Simultaneously*:)

LADY AND LORD.	MAN.
BUT YOU'D BE AMAZED HOW SHALLOW SOME PEOPLE CAN BE	YES, YOU'D BE AMAZED HOW SHALLOW THEY CAN BE

LORD. More wine, Charles.

                              MUSIC Out.

(*Pause*)
LADY. With your permission, my lord, I should like to speak to you alone. (The MAN pauses in pouring the wine. SHE will not meet HIS eye)
LORD. Alone? What on earth for?—Forgive me, you could not very well answer that if we were not alone, could you? Charles! You may go. (*The* MAN *bows and exits. There is a pause. It is clear that the* LORD *thinks the* LADY *is warming to* HIM. HE *leans forward intimately*) Well, madam —
LADY. I wish to be frank with you, my lord. I think you followed me from Bath.
LORD. I set out on the same night as your ladyship.
LADY. In the small hours of the morning?
LORD. (*Drinking*) It happened that the hour was early.
LADY. Happened! You are the Prince's friend, I think?
LORD. Many friendships have been lost by being claimed. Let us say an acquaintance.
LADY. At least you are his companion at the tables, for he has spoken of you.
LORD. Favorably, I trust?
LADY. He called you a good loser.
LORD. His Highness has the best of reasons for knowing that.
LADY. You followed me unknown to him, with a purpose of your own. What was that purpose?
LORD. (*Gallantly*) Need we look far for the answer?

LADY. Farther than this room, my lord. You and I are no friends. We need not play at love-making.

LORD. I protest—

LADY. We need not play at love-making, my lord. Now, why did you follow me?

LORD. There is a code of honor that imposes silence in such affairs. (*Fills his glass*)

LADY. I have heard of it. A man's code. It decrees that women shall not be spoken of, but only marketed. A runaway mistress makes her lover farcical.

LORD. The fortunate man who has once pleased you has his pride to consider.

LADY. The Prince, you mean?

LORD. You parted abruptly. Even noticeably.

LADY. And how should we part? Am I to wait until I am forty, to be pensioned off and receive a lodge in a Royal park, where I shall subscribe to charities and keep spaniels? Thank you! I am a plain woman, and will make my own way in life.

LORD. Yet, madam, there are some ways that would clearly be inconvenient?

LADY. For instance?

LORD. For instance, if you should return to the public stage.

LADY. You think I should not be popular?

LORD. On the contrary, madam. Too popular. Your affairs are common knowledge.

LADY. And if I should defy the ban, and return to my profession?

LORD. A means would be found of preventing you. The playhouses are not uncontrolled. I venture to speak in the name of the Court.

LADY. So I am to consider you as an ambassador of the Prince?

LORD. An ambassador without credentials.

LADY. Engaged on a mission that is not without risk?

LORD. Risk, madam?

LADY. What if His Highness should overtake us here?

LORD. Set your mind at rest. We shall be undisturbed.

Act One Scene 7

MUSIC In.

LADY. Undisturbed? I begin to understand you.
LORD. We must pass the night under this roof, my dear. It is better to be friends.

SONG: "With A Friend Like You"

(LORD *sings*)
    I'M THE FRIEND FOR YOU
    SO CONFIDE IN ME, I'LL TRY TO SEE YOU
        THROUGH

LADY.
    ALL MY TRUST I WOULD BESTOW
(*Aside*)
    (JUST AS FAR AS I COULD THROW)

LORD.
    LET ME KNOW I HAVE A FRIEND LIKE YOU

BOTH.
    WITH A FRIEND LIKE YOU

LADY. (*Aside*)
    (BONAPARTE WOULD NEVER NEED A
        WATERLOO)

LORD.
    YOU HAVE SENSE. AM I CORRECT?

LADY.
    EVEN MORE THAN YOU'D SUSPECT

BOTH.
    WHO'D EXPECT TO FIND A FRIEND LIKE YOU.

LADY.
    SO OUR FRIENDSHIP IS YOUR PLAN, SIR.

LORD.
    MY DEAR, WHAT'S YOUR ANSWER?

LADY.
    NOTHING COULD BE DAFTER
    I KNOW WHAT YOU'RE AFTER—

(*Speaks*) You will oblige me, my lord, by ceasing to drink in my company.
LORD. This is a common tavern, I think.

LADY. But I am not a common woman.
LORD. Indeed?
LADY. You dare to speak of friendship! You, of all the fops and toadies who corrupt this world. You, the philosopher of the green tables! The pimp of fashion, the cold heart of debauchery! You, the very darling of your dicing, drinking, lecherous set! Ha!
LORD. Be careful, madam, you're making an enemy.
LADY. (*Sings*)
>   WITH A FRIEND LIKE YOU
>   WHO WOULD MIND TO HAVE AN ENEMY OR TWO?
>   LITTLE LAMBS IN LITTLE PENS
>   ALL THE LIONS IN THEIR DENS
>   WOULD BE QUICK TO MAKE AMENDS
>   AND THEY'D ALL BECOME GOOD FRIENDS
>   IF THEY ONLY HAD A FRIEND—LIKE YOU?
>   Ha!

MUSIC Out.

(SHE exits up stairs)
LORD. Vixen! Actress! (Fumes awhile, crosses left) Charles! Charles! (The MAN enters right)
MAN. My lord?
LORD. I have use for you, Charles. Listen! (The LORD approaches) This fine lady has had the effrontery to call me a toady.
MAN. Surely your lordship is mistaken.
LORD. No, that very word. Toady!
MAN. Is such ingratitude possible?
LORD. It rankles, Charles. We must prepare a revenge to meet the case. And that is where you will help me.
MAN. I, my lord?
LORD. You, my leveler. You shall be her lover.
MAN. I—her lover?
LORD. Yes, you shall woo this high-stepping beauty, arid bring her to her knees.
MAN. I dare not presume so much.
LORD. Why, man, you have a figure like the rest of us, and

the wit to play at honesty. I swear I could believe in you myself.

MAN. My lady may not be so easy.

LORD. I'll answer for her. Who is she, at the best? A common singer who has climbed the back stairs of fortune! I vow that anyone can have her for the asking.

MAN. (In spite of himself) Your lordship speaks too freely of this lady.

LORD. Ah! That tone is better. Chivalry, Charles—there's the note to strike.

MAN. I'm but a servant.

LORD. True, she may have her pride. Show her that you have yours. You shall not suffer, Charles. And I shall see that you are handsomely rewarded. Name what sum you please. will you do my errand, or at least attempt it?

MAN. (*After a pause*) I am at my lord' s command.

LORD. (*Who is drinking heavily*) Good. Very good.

MAN. Your lordship, I hope, will give me the benefit of your advice.

LORD. (*Thinking*) Hmmmm—Speak of me—none too kindly, for she hates me.

MAN. I will not speak ill of your lordship.

LORD. Have no scruples. Say your worst.

MAN. I would rather rely on my own merits than on your lordship's shortcomings.

LORD. Very shrewd! Yes, you have the finer touch.

MAN. Thank you, my lord.

LORD. But do not be too respectful. A gentlemanly ardor will do no harm.

MAN. A manly ardor.

LORD. Manly may be better. You have it all at your fingertips. Why should I presume to instruct you?

MAN. Your lordship is a person of great experience.

LORD. Well—Yes—Play the gallant rescuer—that should go well. Then the groom with a soul above your station— a sure card. Perhaps even the gentleman in disguise—

if that plot is not too threadbare.
MAN. I would prefer something fresher, my lord.
LORD. You may be right. We should avoid the rut.—You will contrive a message and a meeting. She left a glove in her carriage. Send that to her.
MAN. Isn't that a bit direct, my lord?
LORD. No half measures, Charles. Press the advantage to the end. Do not spare her!—But a gentle beginning would be best.

MUSIC In.

"Wayside Inn" THEME

(LORD *Sings*)
    THE HOUR IS LATE
    THE INN IS STILL
    DON'T HESITATE
    EXPRESS YOUR WILL
    YOU MUST BE WARM
(*Spoken*) Even compulsive
(*Sings*)
    BUT NOT TOO WARM
(*Spoken*) That's repulsive.
(*Sings*)
    THE RIGHT WORD WHISPERED IN HER EAR
    AND YOU WILL CONQUER, NEVER FEAR
(*Speaks over the concluding bars of MUSIC*) Study your lover's part, for you shall play it within the hour! (MAN *exits center.* MAID *enters left, carrying candle*)
MAID. Your pardon, my lord.
LORD. (*Crossing down*) There is my runaway. Well, are you content with your lodging?

MUSIC Out.

MAID. Indeed I am, my lord. If we could meet such gentlemen as you every day—
LORD. There. (HE *blows out* HER *candle*) You are safe with me. (*Pulls* HER *to* HIM, *kisses* HER, *and whispers in* HER *ear*)

Act One   Scene 7   45

MAID. (*Breaking away*) Fie, my lord, fie! What do you take me for?
LORD. I take you for a pretty woman who knows how to be discreet. Am I right?
MAID. But —
LORD. No buts. My door will be on the latch. Are we agreed?
MAID. Perhaps.
LORD. Ah!
MAID. I said perhaps.
LORD. The word— (Lights HER *candle with candles on the table*)
—of promise. (*Kisses* HER *and goes to the stairs*) And so—presently. (Exits upstairs with candles from table.)

MUSIC In.

(MAID *waves goodbye to* LORD *then crosses down. Traveler closes.* MAN *enters left "in one".* HE *carries lantern*)
MAN. This glove was left by your lady in her coach. Will you take it to her room as you pass?
MAID. (*Taking it*) I will say that you sent it.
MAN. You need not.
MAID. But I will. Pleasant dreams, man. (MAID *exits right. Lights fade. Left alone, the* MAN *smiles ironically. MUSIC starts softly, building slowly. When* HE *begins to sing, it is soft and thoughtful, grows in feeling and strength*)
MAN. A woman wished me pleasant dreams.

SONG: "Come To The Masquerade"
(*Sings*)
      THE MUSIC IS PLAYING,
      THE DANCE HAS BEGUN
      THE LIGHTS ARE BEGINNING TO FADE
      THE MUSIC IS PLAYING
      SO COME EV'RY ONE—
      COME TO THE MASQUERADE!
      IT'S TIME TO GET DRESSED
      IN A FANCY DISGUISE;

IT'S TIME FOR THE JOKES TO BE PLAYED
SO PUT ON YOUR BEST—
WEAR STARS IN YOUR EYES—
COME TO THE MASQUERADE!
COME BE THE JESTER, COME BE THE KING
COME BE THE LOVER WHISP'RING OF SPRING,
COME SING A LOVE SONG; PLAY YOUR GUITAR
COME AS YOU LIKE—BUT NOT AS YOU ARE

(*Start dissolve into garden. Blues up above curtain, amber on* LADY *standing on stairs*)

THE MUSIC IS PLAYING
THE DANCE HAS BEGUN
SO HURRY AND JOIN THE PARADE!
THE MUSIC IS PLAYING
BEFORE IT IS DONE
HURRY AND RUN—
JOIN IN THE FUN—
COME TO THE MASQUERADE
COME TO THE MASQUERADE!

(*Dim-out, ambers on* MAN. MAN *exits left.* **MUSIC** *continues:*)

Scene 8

That night. The Garden

Traveler opens. Complete the dissolve. That night. The LADY *is alone. The* MAN *enters. There is silence as* THEY *look at each other. Finally the* LADY *speaks.*

                                        MUSIC Out.

LADY. The hours passed, and I lay awake. (HE *does not respond*) My maid is not in her room. This inn creaks with misgiving. It is full of stratagems and mysteries. I must know the truth.

MAN. Here you will find nothing but riddles.

LADY. Still the philosopher. You spoke to me as a friend. I thought I could trust you. And yet—you may be in league with your comic lord.

MAN. Friendship is frankness. Do as I advise.

LADY. And that is?

MAN. Return to your room and sleep. If we dig and dig, we shall find too much.

LADY. I am not afraid. I accept all that life offers.

                                        MUSIC in.

I hold out open hands to greet sincerity. (SHE *holds up* HER *gloved hand. Slight pause*)

MAN. No one has spoken such words to me before.

LADY. But I speak them.

MAN. The words are yours. The thoughts are mine. (*The "MASQUERADE" THEME swells up and* HE *takes* HER *in* HIS *arms and* THEY *waltz. MUSIC continues under dialogue*) Do you know that I love you?

LADY. But my friend, my friend—it cannot be.

MAN. So friendship is one thing and love another?

LADY. I did not dream of love between us.

MAN. Nor did I. I awoke, and it was there. I was alone, and suddenly we were together.

LADY. My friend, I think you speak in earnest.

MAN. I have loved you from the first hour.
LADY. At Drury Lane? Is it possible?
MAN. I stood in waiting. A door was opened and you passed.
                                                    MUSIC Out.
LADY. This courtship touches me. (*Suddenly a warm laugh*) Tell me, are we to marry and breed philosophers?
MAN. There are worse brats.
LADY. True, they might be gentlemen-in-waiting. Or—
MAN. Or their servants, you would say.
LADY. You are too conscious of your trade.
MAN. Because your head swims at the thought of the gulf between us.
LADY. I think there is hatred in your love. Confess it—love for the woman—hatred for the plaything and the mistress that I have become.
MAN. No. we have both been waiting for this day. (*The MUSIC swells up as* HE *takes* HER *in* HIS *arms and* THEY *dance again. This time* SHE *breaks away*)
                                                    MUSIC Out.
LADY. Too much has happened since you stood in waiting at Drury Lane—I not knowing of your love. Too many arms have held me since them.

SONG: "Man With A Load Of Mischief"
(LADY *sings*)
> A MAN CAN SAY "I LOVE YOU"
> AND SWEAR A SOLEMN VOW
> BUT THEN YOU FIND HE'S MERELY
> A MAN WITH A LOAD OF MISCHIEF
> A MAN CAN SAY "FOREVER"
> BUT ALL YOU KNOW IS "NOW"
> AS TIME GOES ON HE'S CLEARLY
> A MAN WITH A LOAD OF MISCHIEF
> AND ALL THE THINGS HE TELLS YOU
> YOU'RE LONGING TO BELIEVE IN
> BUT MEN WITH LOADS OF MISCHIEF
> ARE MANY, SOMEHOW
> SOON YOU' LL FIND YOU' RE DANCING

Act One   Scene 8   49

>WITH ANOTHER MAN
>ALL THE WHILE ADVANCING
>FURTHER THAN YOU PLAN
>THEN HE SAYS I LOVE YOU
>WELL, IT MIGHT BE SO
>HOW ARE YOU TO KNOW?
>FOR A MAN CAN SAY "I LOVE YOU"
>AND SWEAR A SOLEMN VOW
>BUT MEN WITH LOADS OF MISCHIEF ARE
>   MANY, SOMEHOW—
>DO YOU STILL LOVE ME NOW?

                                        MUSIC Out.

MAN. Yes—I do.
LADY. What will you ask?
MAN. Yourself.
LADY. Listen, my friend, when a woman has given herself often enough, once more or less makes no matter. But you because we are friends, let us not risk falling out. I cannot give a trifle to such as you.
MAN. I do not ask for trifles.
LADY. Still, I have never given more.
MAN. But I offer more than love.
LADY. No, my friend, you know all that stands between us!
MAN. Your pride speaks there.
LADY. Do not strip me of that.

                                        MUSIC In.

MAN. I would strip our pride from both of us. We have no more to do with it. We have met and spoken; we are two who cannot forget. I will not beg from you. You will give what is in your heart.
LADY. (*Sings*)
>AND ALL THE THINGS HE TELLS YOU
>YOU' RE LONGING TO BELIEVE IN
>BUT MEN WITH LOADS OF MISCHIEF
>ARE MANY, SOMEHOW

                                        MUSIC Out.

(*Speaks*) Who are you—my lover? Who are you, sir? (*Imperiously*) Answer me!

MAN. Shall I tell my lady that I am a gentleman in disguise, in league with my lord? And if I tell you so, will you believe me?

LADY. This world of stratagem! (*Kiss. Silence. MUSIC under*) My heart is worn away. Take what is left of it, and give me yours. I will believe your heart, my lover. (SHE *exits upstairs into the inn*)

SONG: REPRISE - "Come To The Masquerade"

MAN.
>THE MUSIC IS PLAYING
>THE MOMENTS GO BY
>AND I HEAR THE SAME SERENADE
>THE MUSIC IS PLAYING
>AND SAYING HAVE I
>COME TO MASQUERADE?
>A WHOLE WORLD OF LOVERS
>ARE DANCING TILL DAWN
>THEY WHIRL IN A CAREFREE CHARADE
>THOUGH LOVE MAY BE ONLY
>A DANCE UNTIL DAWN
>SOON TO BE GONE
>STILL IT PLAYS ON
>COME TO THE MASQUERADE!

(HE *turns and exits*)

BLACKOUT

MUSIC Out.

(*Traveler*)

END OF ACT ONE

ACT II

(ENTR'ACTE)

Scene 1

The Inn. The next morning.

The "Wayside Inn" theme is heard as the traveler opens. The INNKEEPER *appears, yawning, and very satisfied with* HIMSELF. HE *opens the center door. Then* HE *looks down into the room and sees the table and the remnants of last night's dinner. Music changes theme.*

INNKEEPER. (*Sings*)
    GOINGS-ON, GOINGS-ON, GOINGS-ON —
    WHY IT LOOKS AS THOUGH THERE'S BEEN A
        LITTLE PARTY
(*Speaks*) I vow I was not the least bit wrong when I foretold
    this romance. Ah, to be young and a nobleman! (*Sings*)
    OH, SERVANTS AND MAIDS MIGHT DABBLE
        AWHILE
    BUT NOBLES AND LADIES THEY'VE GOT THE
        STYLE!
    OH, JUST IMAGINE HOW IT MUST HAVE
        BEEN—
    THE LOVELIEST AFFAIR YOU'VE EVER SEEN

SONG: "What Style!"

    HE DRAWS THE SHUTTERS TIGHT
    THE MOON IS OUT OF SIGHT
    THE CANDLES GIVE A LOVELY GLOW;
    SHE SITS A-BLUSHING DEAR
    HE WHISPERS IN HER EAR
    SHE SAYS, "MY LORD, HOW FAR YOU GO!"
    HE ONLY SMILES AT ALL HER GENTLE PLEAS
    HE SAYS, "MY DEAR, YOU ARE A LITTLE

TEASE!"
AT THAT HE FALLS UPON HIS NOBLE KNEES
AND GIVES HER ANKLE JUST A TINY SQUEEZE.

WHAT STYLE! WHAT CHARM! WHAT GRACE!
I'D GLADLY CHANGE MY PLACE
TO BE STYLED IN A STYLISH STYLE
CHARMED WITH CHARMING CHARM
AND BE GRACED WITH GRACEFUL GRACE

SHE TRIES TO RUN AWAY
SHE SAYS, "I MUSTN'T STAY.
I THINK I'LL GO UPSTAIRS AND KNIT."

HIS BLOOD IS SOARING NOW
HIS HEART IS ROARING NOW
MY LORD IS IN A PERFECT SNIT
HE THEN PURSUES HER ALL AROUND THE PLACE
SHE SLIPS AND TEARS A LITTLE BIT OF LACE
YOU'VE NEVER SEEN A MORE EMBARRASSED FACE
NOT HIS, OF COURSE—I MEAN MY LADY'S FACE!
WHAT STYLE! WHAT CHARM! WHAT GRACE!
I'D GLADLY CHANGE MY PLACE

(*Speaks*) There's nothing all that wrong with my place, actually. It's just that, when one gets a little older, one longs for a little graceful grace. (*Sings*)
"OH! NOT SO FAST MY LORD—YOU MUST BE GETTING BORED WHY DON'T YOU SING A LITTLE TUNE?"

"YOU TAKE THE BREATH OF ME, YOU'LL BE THE DEATH OF ME!"
AND THEN SHE FALLS INTO A SWOON.
AS NIGHT IS ALMOST TURNING INTO DAY
HIS FANCY WORDS ARE QUICKLY TOSSED AWAY

Act Two   Scene 1   53

>   AND THEN, INTO THE EVER-MOUNTING FRAY
>   HE CHARGES LIKE A TIGER TO HIS PREY
>   WHAT STYLE! WHAT CHARM! WHAT GRACE!
>   I'D GLADLY CHANGE MY PLACE—

(*Speaks*) Now that I think of it. If I did change my place—I'm not sure I could keep up with the pace. (*Sings*)
>   THEY HURRY UP THE STAIR
>   WITH PASSION IN THE AIR
>   MY LORD IS SHAKING TO THE CORE

(*Slows down, with added innuendo*)
>   THEN FITTING THEIR HIGH STATION
>   ONE LAST HESITATION
>   JUST BEFORE THEY CLOSE THE DOOR
>   TRA LA LA LA LA LA LA LA
>   TRA LA LA LA LA LA LA LA
>   TRA LA LA LA LA LA LA LA
>   TRA LA LA LA LA LA LA LA
>   WHAT STYLE! WHAT CHARM! WHAT GRACE!
>   I'D GLADLY CHANGE MY PLACE
>   TO BE STYLED IN A STYLISH STYLE
>   CHARMED WITH A CHARMING CHARM
>   AND BE GRACED WITH GRACEFUL
>   OH, SO TASTEFUL!
>   NEVER DISGRACEFUL GRACE!

(*At the end of the song, the* WIFE *enters, none too happy at the sight*)

WIFE. (*Indignant*) And so! And so! What clowning is this? (HE straightens himself. SHE comes forward) Are they still a-bed?

INNKEEPER. They are indeed, and small blame to them.

WIFE. My lord and lady can please themselves, but their servants should have been stirring an hour ago. (*Starts off*) I'll rouse them sharp enough.

INNKEEPER. (*Stopping her*) Not so fast, wife. They have the day before them—and we have a week of their company if we make them at home.

WIFE. A week of fiddlesticks! What of the pair of saddle-horses brought during the night?
INNKEEPER. Saddle-horses?
WIFE. I found them tied up behind the barn.
INNKEEPER. Now, how did they manage horses?
WIFE. Never you mind—they managed. And it can only mean that his lordship is planning on leaving us.

INNKEEPER. (*Uneasily*) This is some lovers' quarrel. My lord was too brisk, perhaps. They may make it up. (The MAN enters. The INNKEEPER straightens and turns to HIM) Good morning to you. We were awaiting his lordship's orders.
MAN. Presently. I must first look to the horses.
INNKEEPER. What horses is that?
MAN. Saddle horses that were sent for last night.
INNKEEPER. I know nothing of it.
MAN. Come, Innkeeper. Are there horses here or aren't there?
INNKEEPER. I don't know, I —
WIFE. (*Interrupting him*) You'll find them tied up behind the barn, my man.
MAN. I thank you. (*Exits left*)
INNKEEPER. There's a fellow who could tell a tale if he wished.
WIFE. Yes, and I know just the tale he'd tell. They'll be leaving us by mid-day. There goes your chance for a good profit.

            MUSIC In.
INNKEEPER. (*Dejected*) Oh, dear me! And I did have such hopes of being— (*Sings*)
  STYLED IN A STYLISH STYLE
  CHARMED WITH A CHARMING CHARM
  AND BE GRACED WITH GRACEFUL GRACE
(HE exits left. The LADY enters downstairs. During the course of the song, SHE moves happily about the room. Different music theme in)

Act Two   Scene 1

SONG: "A Wonder"

LADY. (*Sings*)
    YESTERDAY I WAS CLEVER
    YESTERDAY I WAS WISE
    SUDDENLY HE SMILED
    AND I BECAME A CHILD
    AWAITING A MIRACULOUS SURPRISE
    WHEN WE ALL WERE CHILDREN
    EVERY TIME WAS THE FIRST TIME
    SURPRISES ALL WERE MAGICALLY UNFURLED
    AND WE WENT OUR WAY
    AND WE SPENT EACH DAY
    DISCOVERING ALL THE WONDERS OF THE
          WORLD

    LIKE THE GREEN SMELL OF CLOVER RIGHT
          AFTER A RAIN
    A FARAWAY CHURCH BELL
    A WONDER
    OR THE COLOR OF AUTUMN, A RIDE TO THE
          FAIR
    THE MORNING OF CHRISTMAS
    A WONDER
    TO FEEL LIKE THE FIRST TIME
    YOU SAW THE SEA
    OR BONFIRES GLOWING IN THE SNOW
    RUNNING BAREFOOT
    FANCY FREE
    WHEN THE WHOLE WORLD WAS JUST A
          PUPPET SHOW
    BUT OF ALL OF THESE WONDERS, THERE'S
          NONE GREATER THAN
    JUST BEING A WOMAN, A WONDER
    OF ALL OF THESE WONDERS THERE'S NONE
          GREATER THAN
    A WOMAN IN LOVE
    WITH A MAN

                              MUSIC Out.

(*Man enters left*)

LADY. My lover! Take my hand in yours and let us go together.

MAN. What if the Prince should arrive now and claim you?

LADY. I hear no sound of grinding wheels; I see no gouty figure propped among the cushions. That world is dead. My lids are closed. I see you only.

MAN. I can take no dreamer with me. I can take no mistress from cloudland. Your world is there and he is there. This is morning. Wake, woman.

LADY. Woman?—what tone is this?

MAN. The tone of a man who knows that you are woman. The tone of a lover who will have all or nothing.

LADY. Have I not given all?

MAN. No. You have given such favors as a woman grants to a man who pleases her. (*Takes her by the shoulder*) Are you really ready to venture your life—yourself?

LADY. I believe that I am.

MAN. Oh, it should be easy! The doors are opened. The plot is laid for us, the web is spun. Smooth words are all that we need say to one another—words as smooth as kisses. (HE *goes on calmly, but firmly*) I cannot speak them. I cannot play your comedy of love. You think that in this tangle of falsehood, I am true, but I too am false. I must tell you, when I made love to you, it was at my lord's command. You were to stoop to a servant, and put yourself in his power. I can make no excuse, and I will not say I consented to my lord's plan because I loved you—

LADY. No, sir, do not say that! Leave me some pride, I beg of you. Maze within maze of lying! I was ready to go with you! I was ready to trust you!

MAN. Return to Bath in the royal coach that pursues you. In a little while, perhaps, you will smile at the adventure.

LADY. There would have been time enough to tell me!

MAN. I have as much honor as a gentleman—neither more nor less. You see the line of serving men that stretches out behind me. I see the world of ladies to which you

Act Two   Scene 1   **57**

    belong. But which of us can see the day when they will meet and take each other's hands? No. Go back to your own world.
LADY. You know that I shall not go back.
MAN. Your pride again. I too have pride.
LADY. The pride of the lover or the pride of the servant?
MAN. The pride, madam, of a man.
LADY. Then I leave you with it. (SHE exits up stairs)

SONG: "Make Way For My Lady"

                                                MUSIC In.

MAN. (Sings)
    WHEN WILL MOON AND STARS MAKE WAY FOR THE SUNLIGHT?
    WHEN WILL WINTER MAKE WAY FOR THE SPRING?
    CAN A NEW LOVE
    MAKE WAY FOR A TRUE LOVE?
    MAKE WAY FOR MY LADY
    MY LADY AND ME
    WHEN WILL YESTERDAY MAKE WAY FOR TOMORROW?
    WHEN WILL OLD WORLDS MAKE WAY FOR THE NEW?
    CAN THIS 'NEVER'
    MAKE WAY FOR FOREVER?
    MAKE WAY FOR MY LADY?
    MY LADY AND ME
    SHE IS DREAMING; SHE IS PROUD
    I LOVE HER STILL
    WHEN WILL SHE FALL FROM HER CLOUD?
    FALL INTO MY ARMS—AND WILL
    THESE IDLE WORDS MAKE WAY FOR SOME LAUGHTER?
    AND WILL SILENCE MAKE WAY FOR A SONG?
    WHILE I WHISPER WORDS OF PRIDE AND OF DOUBTING

> INSIDE I AM SHOUTING
> TO HEAVENS ABOVE—MAKE WAY FOR MY
> LADY!
> MAKE WAY FOR MY LOVE!

              MUSIC Out.

(Top of applause...)

              MUSIC In.

At the end of the song, the MAN *starts to exit but the* LORD *enters from stairs, stopping* HIM. *The* LORD *is very hung over)*

LORD. Charles! Thank God. I can always depend upon you at least.

MAN. I think I should tell you, my lord

LORD. Oh, please! Coffee first. Not a word before my coffee. (*Man starts out*) And Charles, you will hurry? (MAN *bows and exits left.* LORD *goes to open door but shies from the sun, crosses down to sit at table.* HE *has a very visible headache. The* MAID *enters brightly*)

MAID. No good morning for me, my lord?

LORD. Good morning, my dear—Is your mistress astir?

              MUSIC Out.

MAID. My lady will be with your lordship presently.

LORD. I hope she passed a good night.

MAID. Your lordship should ask her that yourself.

LORD. Did you hear nothing as you brushed her hair?

MAID. Nothing, my lord. (*Starts to run* HER *fingers through* HIS *hair, but* HE *brushes* HER *hand aside*) I was thinking of you.

LORD. Of me?

MAID. Yes, m'lord. I was remembering last night. (*Puts her arm around his neck but* HE *disengages it*)

LORD. Last night—Oh, oh yes, well —

              MUSIC In.

SONG: "Forget"

(LORD *sings*)
> FORGET—
> CAN' T YOU BE SWEET

Act Two   Scene 1   59

>   AND FORGET—
>   PLEASE BE DISCREET
>   AND FORGET
>   MY PET—FORGET!

(*Spoken*)
Nights are made to be forgotten. (Hands her money. SHE looks at it coldly)
>   PLEASE FORGET
>   DO BE A DEAR
>   AND FORGET
>   TRY TO JUST MERELY
>   FORGET
>   WE MET
>   FORGET!

(*Music continues under dialogue*)

MAID. (*Glancing again at the money in her hand*) Is that all your lordship has to say to me?

LORD. What else would you have me say? This is the morning. Still, we must not be ungrateful. (*Ceremoniously*) Thank you, my dear.

(*Sings*)
>   SO FORGET!
>   THESE THINGS WILL HAPPEN
>   FORGET
>   WE TOOK A NAP IN THE CLOVER
>   BUT NOW—IT'S OVER
>   OH, THE NIGHT
>   WAS DELIGHT—
>   NOW IT'S DAY!

(*Suddenly feels his hangover. Holds his head in pain*)
>   GO AWAY —
>   AND FORGET!!

MAID. Thank you, my lord!!

                                                    MUSIC Out.

(SHE *slams out of the room, dropping the money on the table. The* MAN *enters with the coffee just in time to see this last bit*)

MAN. Your lordship's coffee.

LORD. (*Turning*) Thank you, Charles. (*The* MAN *sets the coffee service*) Well, what news of the conquest?

MAN. I obeyed my lord's command.

LORD. You played the lover—with eloquence?

MAN. Well—

LORD. Come, Charles. I will swear you were eloquent—a furnace of sighs quenched in a torrent of declaration.

MAN. I spoke as the occasion moved me.

LORD. We can none of us do more. But you were bold, were you not?

MAN. Perhaps too bold.

LORD. A good fault. You stood your ground as an equal? You cut the figure of the faithful friend?

MAN. Yes, my lord.

LORD. No flattery, I hope—no fawning on her self-esteem. You were the modest adorer, but not too modest—the humble servant without the cap in hand.

MAN. Your lordship guesses rightly.

LORD. Because I know you, Charles, and I know this woman. She was only to be won by the pretence of candor. There is one key that unlocks every heart, and you were the man to find it.

MAN. I fear your lordship rates me too highly.

LORD. What! You will not tell me that you failed with her?

MAN. My lady perceived the truth behind my make believe.

LORD. The truth! Curse her cunning! These clever women are the plague. So—my plan has miscarried?

MAN. It has, my lord.

LORD. Strange. I would have staked a fortune on your success. And you have passed a lonely night. Have no regrets, Charles. You failed nobly. Perhaps it is better so.

MAN. Your lordship thinks that my success would have been short-lived?

LORD. Sooner or later she would have found you out. And then—a woman tricked, a woman humbled—such cattle are danger-ous. My scheme was too ambitious. It was too much to hope that my lady would stoop in one

flight from the bedchamber to the kitchen.
MAN. Your lordship is outspoken.
LORD. Have no regrets, Charles. The tender passion is much overrated by the poets. The only lasting pleasures are those of the mind. You are the most excellent of servants, but as a lover— ha! One of us at least upholds the banner of chastity—tattered though it be!!
MUSIC In.
(Claps MAN on the shoulder. Sings)
FORGET
JUST BE A MAN
AND FORGET—
(MUSIC swells up as the LORD yawns, shakes his head and exits right. The MAN watches him a moment, then starts out the other way. The WIFE and INNKEEPER enter, the INNKEEPER stopping the MAN)
INNKEEPER. Excuse me, man. If you don't mind a question.
MAN. Yes—what is it?
INNKEEPER. Would you be knowing—could it be that his lordship is thinking of leaving?

MAN. (*Pause. Looks toward where the* LORD *exited*) He may be leaving—but I doubt that he is thinking of it. (HE *exits.* THEY *stare after him*)
WIFE. Well!—what on earth might that mean?
INNKEEPER. Never you fear, wife. They'll not be leaving us.
WIFE. Just make certain the bill is paid. That's all I say.
INNKEEPER. Would you cast a slur on his lordship?
WIFE. What do you know about his honesty?
INNKEEPER. I know what I know. The lord and lady had a lovers' quarrel, perhaps. But he'll not leave us with money owing.
WIFE. Lovers' quarrel? What do you know about lovers?
INNKEEPER. I didn't do so badly last night, did I? (*Pinches her.* SHE *shoves him away*)
WIFE. Get away from me! 'Tis morning, and this room needs a good straightenin'.

INNKEEPER. (*Sighs and shrugs*) Have it your way, pet. (*Almost drops the coffee pot*)
WIFE. Careful! That's the only silver we have!
INNKEEPER. Sorry, wife.

MUSIC Out.

(HE *knocks sugar bowl off table*)
Ooops!
WIFE. Oh, dear! Can't you do anything properly?
INNKEEPER. I seem to be all thumbs this morning. (HE *gets on knees to pick up sugar*)
WIFE. As usual!

MUSIC In.

SONG: "Any Other Way"

YOU' RE CLUMSY AND YOU' RE MUDDLED IN THE HEAD
YOU NEVER PAY NO MIND TO WHAT I'VE SAID
YOU'RE FUSSY AND YOU'RE GRUMPY
AND YOUR MANNERS MAKE ME JUMPY
AND YOU STAY UP LATE A-DRINKIN'
'TIL YOU COME UPSTAIRS A-STINKIN'
AND TO TOP IT OFF, YOU GRIND YOUR TEETH IN BED

(*Spoken*) You're really not very tidy, Pet. (HE *rises, crosses to mantel, fills pipe*)

BUT I WOULDN'T HAVE YOU ANY OTHER WAY, I SUPPOSE
NOT ANY OTHER WAY, HEAVEN KNOWS
I'M USED TO YOU BY NOW.

INNKEEPER. (*Spoken*) None of your flattery.
WIFE. (*Sings*)

EVEN THOUGH YOU LEAVE SO MUCH TO BE DESIRED, HEAVEN KNOWS
IT'S TOO LATE NOW - I'M TIRED, I SUPPOSE
I 'LL MUDDLE THROUGH SOMEHOW

INNKEEPER. (*Spoken*) You need a rest, that's what.

Act Two   Scene 1   63

WIFE.
    TO LOOK AT, YOU'RE REALLY A SIGHT
    I DON'T THINK YOU'RE ANY TOO BRIGHT
    YOU NEVER DO ANYTHING RIGHT
    BUT I CAN'T SEEM TO PUT UP A FIGHT
INNKEEPER. (*Spoken*) Stick to your guns, Old Dutch. (*Exits with tray*)
WIFE.
    EVEN THOUGH THERE MUST BE MORE TO
        LIFE THAN HIM, I SUPPOSE
    MY FUTURE WOULD BE DIM, HEAVEN KNOWS
        WITHOUT HIM EV'RY DAY
(INNKEEPER *re-enters*. SHE *does not see him at first*)
    THERE MUST BE A MILLION OTHER THINGS
        HE'S NOT HEAVEN KNOWS
    BUT IN THE TIME WE'VE GOT, I SUPPOSE
    THE WAY HE IS IS HOW HE'LL STAY
    BUT I WOULDN'T HAVE HIM
INNKEEPER.
    I WOULDN'T' HAVE YOU
BOTH.
    ANY OTHER WAY
    NOT ANY OTHER WAY!
                                MUSIC Out.

(*At the end of the song,* INNKEEPER *gives* HER *a rose.* SHE *accepts it, then pushes him away, slightly flustered*)

WIFE. Come. Enough of this. If they're staying, then there's work for us to do. (*Goes to wipe table.* MAID *enters*) Well! There she is. Late again—but in time to help us with the morning meal.
MAID. (*Aloof*) I don't feel up to it, thank you.
WIFE. Listen to her, would you! For shame. Your lady will need looking to.
MAID. Oh, she can look to herself, for all I care.
WIFE. Saucy wench!
INNKEEPER. Oh, come on, wife. Don't badger the girl. We can

manage. (INNKEEPER *and* WIFE *exit. The* LADY *enters from the stairs wearing a riding habit.* MAID *is startled, turns suddenly*)

MAID. Oh! My lady!

LADY. The riding-habit surprises you? (*Smiles*) It will be needed for the rest of my journey.

MAID. But your ladyship knows I cannot ride.

LADY. I know that, Louise. You and I are about to part.

MAID. To part! Oh, my lady, my lady, do not leave me here.

LADY. You will be safe enough. Indeed, I think you may be handsomely rewarded, for you will have a tale to tell or leave untold. Our masters are liberal on such occasions.

MAID. My lady, I meant no harm! Overlook it for this once.

LADY. Your room was empty last night.

MAID. Oh, my lady, forgive me! I promise you it is for the last time.

LADY. Can any of us promise so much?

MAID. I swear it!

LADY. Commit no perjuries on my account. (*Starts out. Turns back*) Bring me my cloak when I call, Louise. (LADY *exits into the garden*)

MUSIC In.

(MAID *slaps hands on chair, then picks up* LADY'S *riding hat, then sings*)

MAID. (*Sings*)
ONCE YOU'VE HAD A LITTLE TASTE OF PINK
CHAMPAGNE
YOU JUST DON'T SETTLE BACK AND DRINK
YOUR BEER.
(SHE *throws hat down and crosses down*)

(*TRAVELER closes, LIGHTS dim to spot*)

SONG: "Little Rag Doll"

Act Two   Scene 1   **65**

> WHAT'S BECOME OF MY LITTLE RAG DOLL,
> BUTTONS FOR HER EYES,
> RIBBONS IN HER HAIR?
>
> WHAT'S BECOME OF THOSE LITTLE BLACK
>   EYES?
> ARE THEY ANYWHERE —
> ANYWHERE AT ALL?
>
> WHAT'S BECOME OF MY LITTLE RAG DOLL?
>
> WHAT' S BECOME OF THE GRASSY PLACE,
> WHERE WE SAT AND READ,
> UNDERNEATH THE TREE?
>
> WHAT'S BECOME OF THE LITTLE TOY BED,
> WHERE SHE USED TO BE,
> SMILE UPON HER FACE?
>
> WHAT'S BECOME OF THAT LITTLE DOLL FACE,
> LITTLE PAINTED MOUTH SMILING ONLY FOR
>   ME?
>
> WHAT'S BECOME OF MY LITTLE RAG DOLL,
> AND WHAT'S BECOME OF ME?

BLACKOUT

Scene 2

The Garden, immediately following

Traveler opens, lights up. Immediately after, LADY *enters.* LORD *discovered on.*

LORD. (*Forcing politeness*) Ah! You have brought the sunshine with you, madam.
LADY. Indeed? I dread these mornings when men who have been gallant are so no longer, and women who have been rash must nurse their pride alone. At night we yield to falsehood, but in this pitiless sunlight we see the truth all too plainly.

MUSIC Out.

LORD. (*Suspiciously*) I confess that I am still groping in the dark.
LADY. Your tone to me is cold this morning.
LORD. I fear it was none too warm last night.
LADY. There you do yourself an injustice. Oh, we had words, I know. You were harsh, my lord, and I was unfeeling. But you will not deny the generosity with which you made amends.
LORD. (*Uneasily*) I don't remember—
LADY. Must I remind you? That is not the woman's part. Spare my pride.
LORD. I fail to understand—
LADY. Must I remind you of your courtesy, your delicacy, your ardor —
LORD. My ardor!!

SONG: REPRISE— "Romance"

LADY. (*Sings unaccompanied*)
LAST NIGHT WHEN YOU HELD ME SO CLOSE
IN YOUR ARMS
I SWEAR THERE WAS NEVER A MAN OF SUCH

Act Two Scene 2 67

    CHARMS!
    THE SMILE THAT ENTICES, THE TOUCH THAT
        ENCHANTS!
    OH, WE HAD A LOVELY ROMANCE—
                                MUSIC In.

LORD. (*Spoken*) Romance? What romance? Have you taken leave of your senses, madam?
LADY.
    MY HEART FAIRLY STOPPED WHEN YOU CAME
        WITH MY GLOVE,
    AT LAST I WAS MADLY CONSUMED BY YOUR
        LOVE
    AND GRANTED SUCH FAVORS AS ONE SELDOM
        GRANTS
    HOW CAN YOU FORGET OUR ROMANCE?
LORD. (*Spoken*) I deny it! Will you have the insolence to claim me as your lover?
LADY.
    HOW CAN YOU FORGET OUR ROMANCE?
LORD. (*Protesting*) I—

LADY. (*Sung*)	LORD. (*Spoken*)
SILLY PROTESTATIONS ARE ABSURD	
	Shameless creature!
HOW WILL YOU DENY YOUR LOVER'S WORD?	
	This is monstrous!
WHY IS IT THAT YOU ARE NOW SO COLD?	
	Why, you vixen!
WHEN LAST NIGHT YOU ACTED UNSPEAKABLY BOLD!	
	Play actress!

LADY.
>YOU WON ME COMPLETELY WITH MANY A
>>KISS
>YOU CONQUERED MY HEART IN ONE MOMENT
>>OF BLISS
>IF YOU SEND ME BACK TO THE PRINCE,
>>THERE'S A CHANCE
>I JUST MIGHT PROCLAIM OUR ROMANCE!

LORD. (*Spoken*) Heavens! We'll both be ruined!

LADY.
>I SWEAR I WILL SHOUT IT—
>THE PRINCE WILL NOT DOUBT IT—
>I SWEAR I WILL SHOUT —
>A-HA-HA-HAAA-A-A-A-A-A!
>OUR ROMANCE!
>OUR ROMANCE!
>ROMANCE!
>A-HA- HA-HAAA-A-A-A-A-A
>OUR ROMANCE!
>OUR ROMANCE!
>ROMANCE!
>ROMANCE!
>ROMANCE!
>ROMANCE!
>ROMA-A-A-A-ANCE!

>>>>MUSIC Out.

LORD. I will swear my innocence!

LADY. That would indeed be chivalrous. But what if I confessed? The Prince would never believe you.

LORD. All who know me will accept my word.

LADY. Your word of honor, my lord, against a woman's avowal of her guilt? We shall see. Remember, one word in the Prince's ear, and I am rid of you both. I leave you to order pistols for daybreak, as great gentlemen do on such occasions.

LORD. But I might happen to kill the Prince!

Act Two   Scene 2   69

LADY. Have no fear, my lord; I will not claim you. You shall kick your heels in the Tower alone.
LORD. So this is a woman's honor!
LADY. We fight with the weapons that come to hand.
LORD. (*Considers a moment*) Very well, madam. If I own myself beaten—what are your terms?
LADY. Terms, my lord?

LORD. Come, we understand each other. I will make an offer. You shall be safely escorted to London.
LADY. Indeed? And safely hidden there, no doubt?
LORD. Willingly.
LADY. And housed and fed? And carried to Dover, and put aboard the packet?
LORD. As you please.
LADY. And who, pray, will be my escort?
LORD. My servant can be trusted.
LADY. (*Disdainfully*) Your servant!
LORD. I have had occasion to confide in him before now.
LADY. You have entrusted him with—delicate missions, no doubt?
LORD. Often.
LADY. And he has never failed you?
LORD. I assure you, madam, that he is the man for your purpose.
LADY. But this man of yours has a romantic character. He has honored me by particular attentions.
LORD. (Pretending surprise) Is it possible? No doubt you put him in his place?
LADY. Yes, my lord. I was able to judge his sentiments at their true value..
LORD. Ha, ha! My luckless Charles! Forgive my laughing, madam, but the fellow's presumption tickles me.
LADY. (Suddenly) You mean he did not tell you—?
LORD. Tell me? Of course, he did. The tiresome details of his failure! My Charles your lover? Ha! I should have split my sides!

                                                    MUSIC In.
(*MUSIC swells up—"A WONDER" THEME. The* LADY *turns and seems to hear the* MAN'S *voice briefly, faintly in the background*)
MAN (*Off*). (*Sings*)
> LIKE THE GREEN SMELL OF CLOVER
> RIGHT AFTER A RAIN
> A FARAWAY CHURCH BELL
> A WONDER —
                                                    MUSIC Out.

(HIS *voice fades. The* LORD *is trying to keep her attention*)
LORD. Madam! Are you listening to me?
LADY. (Turns back, a sudden smile) What—? Oh, yes, my lord!
LORD. Yes—As I was saying—he will be the perfect escort.
LADY. It seems that your lordship is bent upon throwing us together at all costs.
LORD. Come, I vow on my honor that you can trust him.
LADY. But can I trust myself, my lord?
LORD. (*Suspicious*) Madam?
LADY. When my heart is once given, there is no turning back. (*The* MAN *enters stops short*)
MAN. My lord!
LORD. Well, Charles?—You may speak, man.
MAN. My lord, the Prince's coach—it comes this way.
LORD. (*Turning pale*) Impossible! He should be in Oxford.
MAN. The coach turned back at the cross-roads. It will be here presently.
LORD. And all our horses lame! I am lost. (*To the Lady*) If he discovers you here with me, he will suspect the worse. (*Thinking hurriedly*) No, no! Listen to me. Are you prepared to fly on foot?
LADY. If need be, yes.
LORD. The need is desperate. The Prince must not find you here! Charles, you will prepare to convey this lady safely to London. I will give you a letter to my cousin, who will keep her hidden. Travel by what means you

Act Two   Scene 2   71

can discover. I will join you in three days. You understand me?
MAN. I understand, my lord.
LORD. Pen and paper—Ah! My saddle bag. I will write instantly. (HE *exits right, hurriedly. The* MAN *and* LADY *look at each other a moment.* HE *smiles gently*)
MAN. Well, my lady —
LADY. Strange, how lovely these simple, country inns can be.
MAN. Very strange.
LADY. (*Pretending to be arch*) So—I am to go with you after all, if his lordship has his way?
MAN. Fate plays peculiar tricks, my lady.
LADY. (*Stops short*) No, I think it is you who have been playing the tricks.

MUSIC In.

You are something like the man in the sign—only you come bearing a different load of mischief.
MAN. My lady?
LADY. (*Sings*)
    A MAN WHO SAID "FOREVER"
    WHEN ALL I KNEW WAS "NOW"
    AT LAST I SEE YOU CLEARLY
    MY MAN WITH A LOAD OF MISCHIEF
I see now you were only after the truth. Your voice was harsh. I thought you had betrayed me. I beg your forgiveness.
MAN. The truth was there. I had to make certain we both saw it. How else could we live our lives together?
LADY. (*Sings*)
    AND ALL THE THINGS YOU TOLD ME AT LAST I
        CAN BELIEVE IN—
(THEY kiss)

MUSIC Out.

MAN. There is one final truth to be faced. Soon my lord finds a pair of horses I have placed behind the inn. He takes them for his own discovery. He will urge us to mount and ride away.

LADY. I am ready.
MAN. What is this flight but one more stratagem, one more betrayal of ourselves?
LADY. What would you do?
MAN. Remain here and face the Prince. Declare the truth that we are lovers.
LADY. My friend, let the past sleep. I will not see you slighted by these men whom we despise. Leave them to their dreams. You and I together are awakened. Leave the Prince and followers their world to play with. What are they to us?
MAN. But we cannot leave this falsehood behind. I am no longer a servant; you have released me. I do not obey, and I will not command. Can you face them in the same manner? (WIFE *enters from right, crosses up between* MAN *and* LADY *to center doors*)

MUSIC In.
SONG: "Sextet"

WIFE.
>OPEN THE SHUTTERS AND KINDLE THE FIRE
>GO TO THE CELLAR AND BRING UP THE WINE
>GALLOPING, GALLOPING ROYALTY COMES
>GALLOPING, GALLOPING ROYALTY COMES

LORD. (*Enters from right in a hurry, agitated*) Here is the letter, Charles. Now lose no time. The coach is in sight, not half a mile away. By good fortune, I have found a pair of saddle horses for you. (*To her*) Get ready, Madam! (MAID *enters from stairs*)

WIFE.
>HURRY, HURRY
>HURRY, HURRY
>WHAT AM I DOING JUST STANDING HERE?

LADY.
>SUDDENLY YOU SMILE -SUDDENLY YOU
> SMILE—SUDDENLY

Act Two   Scene 2   73

MAID. (*First line is sung offstage*)
>WHAT'S BECOME OF MY LITTLE RAG DOLL?
(*To* LORD)
>WHAT'S BECOME OF MY LITTLE RAG DOLL?

WIFE.
>HOW DO I WELCOME A PRINCE?
>CAN I BELIEVE IT IS TRUE?
>WHAT DO I SAY TO A PRINCE?
>TELL ME, JUST WHAT DO I DO?
>WHAT DO I SAY TO A PRINCE?

(*Repeat four times*)
>TELL ME JUST WHAT DO I DO?

(Repeat four times)
>THE INN NEEDS A FRESH COAT OF PAINT
>ON TOP OF IT ALL I FEEL FAINT

LADY.
>SUDDENLY

(*Repeat 11 times*)
>SUDDENLY YOU

MAID.
>WHAT DO YOU SAY TO THE PRINCE?
>WILL HE BELIEVE IT IS TRUE?
>WILL HE BELIEVE IT IS TRUE?
>WHAT DO YOU THINK HE WILL DO?
>WHAT DO YOU THINK HE WILL DO?
>I MUST TAKE CARE OF MYSELF!
>WHY SHOULD I BOTHER WITH YOU?

(INNKEEPER *enters from right*)

LORD. (*To Maid*)
>FORGET
>PLEASE BE DISCREET
>AND FORGET
>MY PET
>FORGET

INNKEEPER.
>WHAT STYLE! WHAT CHARM! WHAT GRACE!
>I'D GLADLY CHANGE MY PLACE—
>FOR GRACE!

LORD.
> FORGET! FORGET!
> FORGE-ETT!
> (*Speaks*)
> Good heavens, I forgot. Money. You'll need money.
> (*Exits right.*

MUSIC THEME changes

LADY. I will stay. I can face the Prince. Somehow, with you, I have no fear of the prospect.
MAN. Louise, bring your lady's cloak. (MAID *exits right*)
LADY. What! Are we to go now?
MAN. Now. The will to remain is enough! After all, what are they to us!
LADY. So that was the last stratagem. Laughter comes back again.

SONG: REPRISE - "Make Way For My Lady"

MAN AND LADY. (*"Make Way for My Lady" theme*)
> WATCH US
> AS WE GO BEYOND YOU!
> OUR LOVE WILL GO SOARING
> TO HEAVENS ABOVE

MAN.
> MAKE WAY FOR MY LADY!

BOTH.
> MAKE WAY FOR MY LOVE!

(MAID *enters from right with cloak and crops*)
MAID. (*Helping* LADY *into cloak*) Oh, my lady, my lady.
LADY. This is goodbye, Louise. Take my belongings, and remember me kindly.
(LORD *runs on with purse of money which* HE *thrusts in the* MAN'S *hand*)
INNKEEPER AND WIFE.
> STAND ASIDE!
> AND BID THEM FAREWELL

Act Two   Scene 2   75

    WATCH THEM
    AS THEY GO BEYOND US
    THEIR LOVE WILL GO SOARING
    TO HEAVENS ABOVE

LORD. Charles! Here is practically the last of my money. Use it carefully—but for heaven's sake! Hurry! (LORD *runs up to center doors to check the arriving coach.* MAN *laughs and tosses the money to* MAID, *and tears up the letter.* HE *catches up the* LADY *and kisses* HER *again. The* LORD *turns back down to just catch the last of this, his mouth open in surprise.* MAN *draws himself up and waves the* LORD *aside*)
MAN. Stand aside, my lord, (*Sings*)
    MAKE WAY FOR MY LADY!
(*The* LORD *obeys mechanically, almost in a state of shock. The* MAN *and the* LADY *exit right, hand in hand, almost running.* WIFE *and* INNKEEPER *follow them off. The* MAID'S *tears turn to laughter. The MUSIC continues*)
LORD. Did he kiss her? Am I in my senses?
MAID. They have gone away together, my lord! She has found the way.
LORD. He ordered me—ordered me to stand aside! Can you fathom it? (*Notices the torn letter. Picks up a scrap of it*) Am I tricked?
MAID. (*Merrily*) They are in love, my lord! (*Opens the bag of money and tosses a handful of coins in the air*) In love!!
LORD. What are you doing? Stop that! What do you mean in love? (*Aghast*) Innkeeper! Innkeeper! In love? Innkeeper!!! (INNKEEPER *and* WIFE *enter right*) Stop those runaways!!
INNKEEPER. They are gone, my lord. They are over the hill by this time.
(*The 'hill" is at the back of the theatre.* THEY *peer at it across the footlights*)
WIFE. Do you not see them? They are laughing together! Oh, how I love a daring romance!

LORD. Laughing! How dare they laugh! (WIFE *turns up, crosses to center doors;* INNKEEPER *exits right for reckoning*)

SOUND: Musical "coach horn" Oh, my God! The Prince! (HE *grabs the* MAID) Listen to me, girl. This tale may not be believed. The Prince may suspect that I have conveyed that woman away for my own purposes.

MAID. And so, my lord?

LORD. And so you will tell his highness what passed between us last night. I could not very well be making love to you both. Keep my purse, girl. Can I depend upon you?

MAID. No, my lord! You cannot! (*Strikes* HIM *across the face and tosses away the rest of the money*)

LORD. Hell-cat! (INNKEEPER *re-enters with reckoning, puts it in* LORD'S *hand*) What is that?

INNKEEPER. (*Crossing to center doors*) Your lordship's reckoning.

LORD. (*Down center*) What?! Am I to pay for this madness?

INNKEEPER. (*Coming back down*) My lord, it is a privilege of a man of quality.

WIFE. (*At the entrance,* SHE *does an elaborate curtsy, throws doors open*) His royal highness!

(THEY ALL *turn to the entrance. The "WAYSIDE INN" THEME swells up, lights dim, traveler closes*)

END OF MUSICAL

www.ingramcontent.com/pod-product-compliance
Lightning Source LLC
Chambersburg PA
CBHW031414040426
42444CB00005B/569